THE INVENTION OF THE ZERO

RICHARD KENNEY

THE INVENTION OF THE ZERO

ALFRED A. KNOPF

NEW YORK 1993

THIS IS A BORZOI BOOK
PUBLISHED BY ALFRED A. KNOPF, INC.

Poetry magazine first published "Lucifer" and "The Encantadas," excepting sections 10, 11, and 12, which appeared subsequently in *Verse*. "The Invention of the Zero" and "Typhoon" were published in *The New England Review / Bread Loaf Quarterly*. The author is especially grateful to the editors of these magazines—for space, in view of the four poems' length, and for these awards: from *Poetry*, the Frederick Bock Prize (1983, for "The Encantadas"), and the Oscar Blumenthal Prize (1992, for "Lucifer"), and *The New England Review / Bread Loaf Quarterly* Narrative Poetry Prize (1984, for "The Invention of the Zero"). In 1985, "Lucifer," in an early, unpublished form, was awarded the Poetry Society of America's John Masefield Award. "Typhoon" was nominated for a Pushcart Prize in 1991.

James Merrill candled earth first. David Shields gave me good advice. I am no scientist, and have relied on others at every turn: among many, Mary Hedberg, Max Hommersand, Edward Barry, B. Lippitt. Rob Weller conjured the manuscript from chaos to astronomy, and cheered me greatly along the way. Jorie Graham agreed the salutation might be comfortable among the author's other archaisms. Those contributing most substantially to the "matter" of the book are named in the afterword.

Particular and grateful acknowledgements are due the John Simon Guggenheim Foundation, the American Academy and Institute of Arts and Letters in conjunction with the American Academy in Rome, and the Fellows Program of the John D. and Catherine T. MacArthur Foundation, for grants over the last decade which have made a great deal of difference to me and my family.

Library of Congress Cataloging-in-Publication Data

Kenney, Richard.
    The invention of the zero : poems / by Richard Kenney.—1st ed.
        p. cm.
    ISBN 0-679-41991-8
    ISBN 0-679-74997-7 (pbk.)
    I. Title.
PS3561.E443I5 1993
811'.54—dc20

                                                                            92-54790
                                                                            CIP

Manufactured in the United States of America
First Edition

for JAMES MERRILL

CONTENTS

*

Sing,
orbiter, O
with your glassy sun-
flung wing
and glittering eye,
what do you see? What
bitter seed
blooming?

*

Bit by pixel
I see this: guest
stars blooming,
flame to wick:
a future's afterimage
match-lit—

*

☾

♂

☿

♃

♀

♄

☉

*

And do you notice
pattern in it,
orbiter, O
antennae'd tin-
horn, hunter, our
own, orienting dark-
ward, quirt back
to blank heaven
and the prickly heat
of stars?

*

The pattern's partial,
Lord, its pointillism
incomplete: to plot
this form
requires more flame:
this is still
a constellation
without a name.

*

4

Ø

A Colloquy of Ancient Men

1

In the beginning was the

word comes weird. . . . After

2

AE: world. . . . The Lord God does not play dice with the

JRO: worlds. . . . We waited until the blast had passed, walked out of the shelter and then it was extremely solemn. We knew the world would not be the same. I remembered the line from the Hindu scripture, the Bhagavad-Gita: Vishnu is trying to persuade the Prince that he should do his duty and to impress him he takes on his multi-armed form and says *Now I am become Death, the destroyer of*

CD: World monkeys; and from the latter, at a remote period, Man, the wonder and glory of the universe, proceeded. . . . The Simiadae then branched off into two great stems, the New World and the Old

JC: world was to be finally accomplished by a catastrophic disturbance of the atmosphere, he would have assimilated the information under the simple idea of dirty weather, and no other, because he had no experience of cataclysms, and belief does not necessarily imply comprehension. The wisdom of his country had pronounced by means of an Act of Parliament that before he could be considered as fit to take charge of a ship he should be able to answer certain simple questions on the subject of circular storms. . . . Had he been informed by an indisputable authority that the end of the

IN: world; but to myself I seem to have been only like a boy playing on the seashore, and diverting myself in now and then finding a smoother pebble or a prettier shell than ordinary, whilst the great ocean of truth lay all undiscovered before me. . . . I do not know what I may appear to the

[Albert Einstein; J. Robert Oppenheimer; Charles Darwin; Joseph Conrad; Isaac Newton; James Jeans; Arthur Stanley Eddington; Max Planck; Bernard le Bovier de Fontanelle; Herman Melville; Neils Bohr; Fred Hoyle; J.B.S. Haldane; Mark Twain.]

AE: world. . . . Physical concepts are free creations of the human mind and are not, however it may seem, uniquely determined by the external

JJ: world into a more rational shape in our

3

minds than the shape into which it is thrown there by the crude order of our experience. . . . indomitable desire to cast the world into a more rational shape in our

ASE: mind may be irrational, and we can never succeed in formulating them. . . . It is even possible that laws which have not their origin in the

MP: minds, but eventually die. . . . Scientist never change their minds, but eventually die. . . . Scientists ne

4

BBF: ver died. . . . As long as roses could remember, no gardener e

HM: ver contracting towards the buttonlike black bubble at the axis of that slowly wheeling circle, like another Ixion I did revolve. . . . Round and round, then, and e

NB: veryday language, we can only hope to grasp the real facts by means of these images. . . . Quantum theory thus provides us with a striking illustration of the fact that we can fully understand a connection though we can only speak of it in images and parable. . . . since we can only describe natural phenomena with our e

FH: verse. . . . Grant me the hydrogen atom, and I will deduce the uni

JBSH: verse is queerer than we think. The universe is queerer than we can

5

HM: think that the Problem of the Universe is like the Freemason's mighty secret, so terrible to all children. It turns out, at last, to consist in a triangle, a mallet, and an apron,—nothing more! And perhaps, after all, there is *no* secret. We incline to

AE: thinking, and we thus drift toward unparalleled catastrophes. . . . The unleashed power of the atom has changed everything save our modes of

thinking. . . . The whole of science is nothing more than a refinement of our everyday thinking. . . . The whole of science is no

HM: thing more! We incline to think that God cannot explain His own secrets, and that He would like a little information upon certain points himself. We incline to think that God cannot explain his

6

ASE: own. . . . We have found a strange footprint on the shores of the unknown. We have devised profound theories, one after another, to account for its origin. At last we have succeeded in reconstructing the creature that made the footprint. And lo! it is our

JRO: own sin, and this is a knowledge which they cannot lose. . . . In some sort of crude sense which no vulgarity, no humor, no overstatement can quite extinquish, the physicists have kn

MT: own much darkness on this subject, and it is probable that, if they continue, we shall soon know nothing at all about it. . . . The researches of many commentators have thrown much darkness

7

was on the face of the deep. . . . In the beginning was the ses. . . . I frame no hypotheses.

9

*

The seas achieved
thee, orbiter, spit
pearl turned
and turned against flecked
velvet for thy
own vain joy:
reflect a moment on that hissing conch-
shell, self-
consciousness, last exhibit
in the last vitrine
in the Great Hall of Fishes,
wave-lapped, duneless sand-
glass where the first sea
keeps an open line,
returning its own call
to its shell-
bone, brine self: *receive*
receive

*

Is this the salt
root of the Great Tree—
thralled God's—
girdled now, and green crown
dowsing?
Count down:

*

*

Then mind made
heaven . . . heaven
seeks ⦶—vor-
tex, thyr-
sus-struck—to . . .
winnow?—no:
Then innate
heaven zigs
fire forth re:
deuton's wand,
one

*

O
send some sun
sign, Father!—
thee, far-
thrower: thyrsii
bloom not once upon a time
I think, if future is a branching
tree: that I see nothing thus
far in the flame names
not that nothing: frame
thy own hypotheses.

*

*

Or where are traces of the future?
Siva the Destroyer, then?
or *Lucifer, Le Cyffre?*
The Sieve? The Scythe?
The Girdled Stem?
Riddle me a riddle, O: if
not these, then—

*

Solve sky thyself,
Father, earth's
aleph, all of
it: O Maker! Vulcan!
candle heaven if
you can: tell
then of the first egg,
the omega then, x,
y, and what befell:

*

*

This is the story
my people tell:
we close the fist and say
*Everything in the
shape of nothing.
This is the darkness
before physics.*
We open the fist:

*

Lo!
first starlight's
slow vermiculation
through the asphalt
fall of empty space,
syntax of the free quarks
all around, arrayed now
at the radio's farthest
static rim: ring
now, noctilucent wake,
wave-weft, particle, O,
the world's one ancestral sky
skull-capped here, and come
back to its senses . . .

*

The Invention of the Zero

We knew the world would not be the same. I remembered the line from the Hindu scripture, the Bhagavad-Gita . . . .

In some sort of crude sense which no vulgarity, no humor, no overstatement can quite extinguish, the physicists have known sin, and this is a knowledge which they cannot lose.

X-rays leaking from a black hole, let's say, limn
these bones, Dear Reader: soft and stirring, embryos
blown forward through all time to come, like a sudden aria
of soap bubbles, dozens at a breath, or an hour's exposure
of the moon's eclipse: *ring, ring, ring,* lamplight
flaring on the lens—

> The sun's the real plot-
line here, of course. My role—Apollo's, chariot
and all (a Chrysler), in reverse: first tincture
of the photochemical response: aurora
oriented west, once, and the world changed . . .

> Withershins:
begin, accelerating eastward through foreshortened
headlight, dim at ninety miles an hour, land tec-
tonic, slipping past at either side, torn chintz
in ragged folds in the middle ground, and earth-
shine silver overhead—

> Ahead, the far shore
draws the mind on the neap outflow of frail Atlantic
tide, let's say, where stars will slip back in
again—

> *Gone West* we say, following the ortho-
doxy of the sun's own hemisphere,
its track and disappearance there, the stone's throw
off the California coast, where I began
this drive (as once before, some years the other
way)—and what's to come? As if the sun might misfire,
fail to rise one day! What do I know? *M* is for
mass, and *E* the awful energy that beckons
from inside it (oh, and flickers in our leaders'
eyes!) like firelight through a stone scrim . . . the speed
of light's another thing. Night now. The semaphore
of starlight winking overhead while the nearer beacon's
blacked out, blinked out, filtered through the zillion liters
of liquid stone yolk and granite mantle and broken
crust where the planet's come between—

> Protective disk,
the veil of film held up to each mundane, parochial
eclipse, called *night.* Imagine this: a slight bleed
of shadows through it, oil-drop through the flat statistics-

19

sheet this quantum world is said to be—blank keyhole,
tumblers, *tic, tic,* all space itself in pleats
and folds, and light sucked back around a flat accretion
disk such singularity attracts, all axes
bent to pretzels—what a world! Why not an X-
ray of the earth, then, pinned beside the Pleiades
at night, like so, a black hole *here,* a gauzy creche
here, where stars still reproduce their subtle lattice-
works of ones and zeroes, lacing blue creation
into form—

○

2
Magic
Lantern

　　　　　Acetylene! Touched torch! An orange
ball, and all life candled on its memory:
arranged so, earth held up between such satellites
as *sun,* as *eye,* high noon between the Atlas Range
and Madagascar, drifting west, and nightfall settled
here on my stooped shoulders like a black box-camera's
cape, squeeze-bulb in my hand, scintilla
set to powder in the instant *still, still*—
O say, what might I see? See land limned
in a whey of white stone falling to the seafloor, chyme
and lymph and salt and pulse-beat just off-center, sun
before me, rinsed in photographic chemicals,
resolving, moon behind me, yellow, lit like a lemur's
great eye and rising, casting whose chimeric
shadow down to merge with a mirror-image?—*mark:*
before the stopped film burns through, curls
back, catching fire, the whole chiaroscuro
gone, the frail electric surface of the North American
Desert disrupted, sand to stained glass in a great scare-
crow cratering, to blind this candled cockerel—

Not dawn. Begin again: choke back these *Kyries*
for now, and spin this tale with all the arrogance
that it requires, beginning with *diaspora,*
while highway reels black asphalt back across this sparse
moonscape like a strip of exposed film, *frame, frame,*
an overlay. And what dark mass appears
off-center in the hot sun-softened field, a fractal

20

shape I recognize, like a shadow on a scanned
lung, cast off the magic-lantern's flame?—
reversed, unclear, this shape (I know) is *Africa*
as seen from underneath—the rafting Ark
where all imagined radiance began,
all shadow-show that plays across the silver membranes
separating us, and light from dark,
and life from memory, as glass from stain—

○

3
False
Dawn

Again: out of one sun setting at my back
and overland the short way toward the next—
a dreamt drive, desert night, and pupils wide
to take it in: *accelerate:* one axis
in a folded map's accordion connects,
and night with night, one thirty years ago I'd
never thought to blink so long—

                     And what I witnessed
then?—that's *history*, I guess, the *Pax
Americana* say, *the sunrise in the West.*
If not the sun, then say its first approximation
on the surface of the earth. You've seen the pictures
of it, surely, *tic-tic-tic,* the film's slow-motion
churning, changing, charring white what cicatrix
still burns a blind spot in the sky's clear retina
tonight—
            Too light! Too late to show the rest—the tint
of false dawn far ahead, resolving in that trick
of light whose afterimage turns, returns,
to show the world again. Begin: a landscape reddened
just at dawn, a spark tossed in its tinderbox,
a powder-flash, one moment pressed into its plate—
a photograph of what's to come?—a silvering
inside the eye?—the flash we still anticipate.

Thus, *genesis:* a drum-roll struck off cinderblock,
a charcoal blacking on the cheeks, a blaze of sulphur
in the nose, and pupils blinking strings of pearl
like full moons into fumaroles. The epicenter
of the sunrise. Amphitheater of fools.

False dawn. Forget it all; the night sky itself's
a grainy image at the best. By chaparrals
beside the road (old as the Presidency) pissants
raise up low revetments; kangaroo rats fill
their cheeks with yucca seed and dodder seed (weak beta
sources still, no doubt); here skinks sleep; sagebrush sows
its meager earth with chemicals to kill invading
tumbleweed. A world of Spanish bayonet,
cattle spinach, salt bush, black brush, creosote;
nothing grand as a Joshua tree. *Nevada
Test Site:* this was 1953, or *Anno
Mundi* who knows what—what zeroes, increate,
remain?—the actuaries off in neon Never-
Never Land could make that book, no doubt, in Reno,
or Las Vegas, shave the odds in secret inks—

                                            And rate

them even?
                No: the silver anniversary
of all of this has come and gone. Tonight, serene,
no motion on the earth but mine, a serrate
ridge of mountains in the distance, desert still,
the playa like a standing pool of starlight
left behind when the last seas receded here
sometime before the Paleocene—before the great
extinctions, say, the last catastrophe. A sterile
silver light left over from a clear
and long-dead star, maybe, irradiating
all this dead desert, now, where the road
threads east to the Utah line—

✸

4
Tar
Pit
                             And too, out there, and dating
us as surely as the cloud-track of the alpha
flying off, ineffable decay, a ring
of light expands out through the spring stars,
whose source is cooling here. Begin again: I started
in Los Angeles—or say LaBrea, where asphalt
bubbles up across the crust, carcasses
and caught grotesques tossed back to light again: the tar pit
tipped downhill across the tilting and distorted
plate of North America, to slip its faults

and basins like some buzzard's flystrip, dotted, car-
strewn, crows lifting and settling over it, and seized
in turn—
           Or so it seemed, in the heat of the afternoon,
at ninety miles an hour through the dead Mojave
marking towns like *Chloride, Searchlight, Mercury;*
the road seemed a single point extruded east
into this line, between the tides of sun and moon . . .
inside, the saline blood responds: the same heavy
waters dragged once, after all, across the murk
and sediment of this dead ocean's floor, and we feel
it still, maybe, the slip of shadows, the slow shape
of the armored fish that glides across the road ahead,
that glides across the mind—

                        What North America
tonight, between the sine wave of some simple eel
and the sun's last x-rays cooling on the nape?
What change! The pitchblende ticking down to lead,
the watchfob spinning through its phases, *mark*
and *mark* and *mark*, the pulse inside the ribcage creel,
the sequence of the dying heart—

                    ○

5   Our neighbors
Romance   in Arcturus and the Lesser Magellanic
Cloud will count these pulses through the dark,
the first ignition of the strobe, and guess what grail
we've stumbled on, umbrageous, such bright tapers:
Upshot, Knothole, Teapot, Plumbob—matchlight,
hand-cupped, licking in the tinder of the Ark
(or each, more technically, a *Plowshare Cratering
Event*—evincing, neither here nor there, the torpor
of official prose, applied to magics
of the very highest order). Arcane
work by any name; though later, guttering
in green light on the desert's vitrified *parterre,*
the fireworks (as befits such demiurgical
occasions, in a place like Frenchman Flat) were marked
by more romantic names, *viz. Palanquin,
Cabriolet,* and *Schooner,* and *Sedan* . . . Peut-être

                    23

too Romantic, yet—the Pantocratering Event . . .
well, this was that, in a manner of speaking, sparks
struck off the steel of time like grains of pollen linking
us to what first awful flowering perturbs
the empyrean still—a style we haven't
truly mastered, high and grand, the first appalling
pyrotechnic, echoing at three degrees above
the zero—
        Oh, tympanic heaven
oscillates to every touch, and call it
what you will, the nonexistent ether
hums, and dimming stars and nebulae like white grease
sleet apart to dead inertia; withershins
all starshine fades, and still the night sky rings like a skillet,
remembering the shock of the first fire—

○

**6
First
Fire**
                                          Earth's
no place for this, I think. And think of fire: begin
again, with Agamemnon's signal lights: five beacons
set on mountaintops (recall them: *Lesbos, Athos,
lost,* and the next, too, *lost,* and *Sounion*—)
to chain the spark from east to west, from flaming Troy
the good news blinked across the sea to the cold hearths
of the Pelopponese: *Word from the warlords of Mycenae* . . .
we receive the message, still. One spark—how soon
it leapt up all horizons, strata, time, destroying—
what?—the grace of Persepolis, the mathematics
of Alexandria, the slow and careful masonry
of even the simplest human dream?

                                   What industry
our species shows! What strange and mad anathemas
we've uttered on ourselves here in this smoky maze
we've made our home, unravelling the single plume
of orange flame whose wick braids up from some dry wadi
somewhere in East Africa, to thread the gloom
of Quattrocento caves, through Attic
lime-kilns, lit cathedrals—each illuminated
mass we've cupped in mind since Quaternary
time began—

The muzzle-flash of History,
indeed. Imagine this, some dim nomadic
hominid who, eating nits and mangoes, squatting
by the shores of Lake Nyasa *circa* what,
three million years B C, let's say, observed his starry
heavens change: a glint in The Hunter's sword: new matter
turned to energy and smeared across the void
as light, to touch the human retina—the quantum
of the rod-and-cone, one impulse in the optic
nerve . . . and lo! A new fire brought to ground.

○

7
Orion   Transmitter
in M-42 still crackling, still devoid
of sense. We've answered all the same, in time, the wands
of power flaming in our palms, *tic-toc,* dropped—

And this is how it was: again, Nevada
Proving Grounds, in 1953, where once
upon a time I was a young man, Airman
First Class X, held under the MP's quick raptorial
gaze at three A.M., waved through the checkpoint, jeep
parked, ushered out to an observation area
near Frenchman Flat or Yucca Flat, rapt
as the rest of the small crowd gathered from its sleep,
assembled on this naked slope by the eerie
floodlight of the moon and the piercing desert stars—

Sparks inside their vacuum tube, they seemed to leap
so, *cathode, anode,* counting down to dawn. No roosters
but beribbonned officers, and stranger birds
among them, easy to distinguish in the opera-
box of the forward zone, reserved for VIP's
and military brass (was Oppenheimer
there? Perhaps he was, a slide-rule scabbard
swinging from his belt, and sabretache
of instruments, binoculars, ah, *Science!* eyepiece
always turning, *tic-tic-tic—*) *Abra-cadabra.*
Agamemnon's shamans, spelling, casting ash
across the night. *A new star—*

25

                                    Orion
would have set by then, in February,
early March, so nearly dawn, the Crab
above him, balancing the dark horizon
to the west; but still I saw that central rhinestone
in his sword, M-42, the Nebula, that brewery
of fresh stars forming, lit not long ago, as these
things go—
                    Again: and numbers, nine to one,
and the edged blade, the lesson taught poor Damocles,
the inner physics of the sun—

                              O

8   Such things
Theory come back. But a host of thoughts afflicted us, no doubt,
those nights, waiting, breath coming in clouds,
speaking softly, the small group of people thronged
together there, recall—it might have been an Easter
sunrise service, almost—all sorts: us, civilians,
officers. . . . There was a levelling of rank
out there. It's hard to say just how it was, those starry
nights. I'd try again, and get it wrong.

Dawn approached, a grey sift in the valley. On
the loudspeaker, the count began. It rivetted
our separate dreams, it synchronized us, then: *ten minutes,*
left, then *five,* then *one,* mark *fifty seconds*—rung
by rung the tower lightened into view. We turned
our backs, as ordered—*forty.* Each of us was fitted
with a special pair of goggles, tight, opaque
as film I'd used as a child to watch my first eclipse
through—*thirty seconds* now, and *twenty seconds, ten,
nine—eight*—

                    What artificial dawn would break
and ring the hardpan like a gong with thunderclaps
that rolled and echoed round and round the mountains'
rims (mark *seven, six*), and sheet the retina
with white fire *(five, four)* and rake
the spine with recognition in this small collapse
of matter of a thing so *alien*

                              26

as makes all former human-scale abominations
seem—how?—*homely* by comparison . . . mark *three,
two*—I was prepared for all of this. The salient
burst at any rate; the clockworks of the bomb
were clear enough to me, I understood the theory
of the thing, the queer unearthly thought, the sleight
of physics balancing its spindly tower there
not seven miles away; and what I knew of sunlight
set me for that first radiant outrush searing
on the nape of the exposed neck between the collar
and the hairline—*one*—when the bomb brushed *zero* . . .

❂

9
Zero

Theory! White light leached all thought, all shade, all color
left the earth the moment first light leaked the seals
around our masks, and night was day—

                                We all whirled
in our places, tore the glasses off, to see—
what—*the world* again, and this part of the world:
it found me unprepared for this: the beauty
of the thing evolving, changing so before our eyes—
for ten or twenty seconds, still, it was a sun-disk,
yellow-white, Ikhnaton's fireball, slowly knurling
at its edges, turbid, losing outline, imbued
bit by bit with color, incandescent, rising
in a great upchurning cloud, first rose-pink, damask
as the reddish desert (which it was) annealing
in its own fire: cyan, rose, a purple, lemon,
a sort of kelly-green: these were the elements
transmuting through excited states. They masked
each other, changing, churning, shimmering in oil-
quick veils across the lobed, swelling minaret
of cloud . . .

                What came to me? *The mind of Ammon-Ra,
an abacus of neutrons clicking in the mosque
where mathematics came to zero: seconds, minutes,
split degrees . . . the atom of uranium,
its tesselated marble floor and fine vaulted
inner shells so delicate, a Ming urn,
and all our ashes cupped inside . . .*

27

                                        So much for *M*,
for *E*, for the speed of light square against the brain pan
then, for constellations wheeling through the psalter
of some lost star-gazing camel-driver's dog-eared
charts, passed on to SAC command, or the Pan Am
navigator winking winglights over white salt
here, another desert, another star's point soldered
to the page, predicted, marked. . . . What auguries
our numbers are!

                              ○

10   Tonight, the tympanum
Bloom   of earth seems all but still, the desert hardpan dampened
in the touch of years, of tires. Camp Mercury
is dead. No checkpoint now; all the old ogres
gone, and the dim Cretaceous gone, its gargoyles
gone; but driving here tonight the sense of the damned
remains, ticking slowly out like curies
through a badge of film pinned against the heart—
                                        Here cars
rocket toward me, lights, rattlesnakes like Argyle
socks, flat crows, flat packrats litter the macadam
like the dead from far LaBrea, and *Kyrie*
we say, we beg our dreams at night for mercy, souls
rattling with fear and shame—
                              And I, here, an arc
of headlight, aimed, accelerated like some atom
toward its last disintegration, carry
all these thoughts, it seems, at once: of quiet missile
fields ahead, the metal rose melting in the lantern
of each slender buried spire . . . automaton
held down by what but white fingers of some curious
gnome inside his granite mountain somewhere, muzzle-
flash flickering his dilate pupils, his own land
lime-sweet on his tongue—

                              I think of Omaha, the autumn
of the Pleistocene unfolding, ocherous
and russet under earth-stained fingers: umbers,
oxides brushed to life, in two dimensions: aurochs,
reindeer, hare, and horse, and mastodon—

                              28

                                        Here Adam's
needle by the roadside, flowering—corrosive
soil so pyrotechnic when it blooms! All embers
blown up flame at once, with the first spring rains. Recall Rock
Valley and the Specter Range, where jeep trails rose
into the hills like fine threads through the light-struck sieve
of rods and cones inside the eye itself—a silver
dropcloth all at once in a night rain's pointillism
lit, all touched to color, so: sweet Chorizanthe,
creosote, and ghost, and sage in yellow sprays,
and red: Verbena, locoweed and Lupine;
blue: wild heliotrope and desert asters—prisms
of them, shattering to seed and sun, the whole display
alive, extinct, in two weeks' time—a short blaze
and broad-cast; done.

                        And in the time-like loop and line
of human consciousness? Who knows how seeds sown
here or there may come to pierce the hardpan playa's
floor again, what annuals' quick-blooming
burst: mark: *Upshot, Knothole, Teapot, Plumbob*—
Lesbos, Athos, lost, lost, and *Sounion* . . .
These are—these have become—the fixed stars' points, the fetch-
lights shining through our dreams.

                            ☼

11   For one last time: the plume
Star-   of flame, the point of dawn, the atmosphere fluorescent
light   in the mind's eye a moment—argon, neon
in a discharge tube, expanding over Frenchman
Flat and Yucca Flat, in one white amnion
of firelight billowing to darkness—
                            Here, the floor
of this forsaken desert sputters, carpeted
with flowers for its instant, sparks (like us) from road-flares
fused and lit (how long ago?)—from neurons
braided up through the brains of tree-shrews, sheared
clean at last like cold lamp-wick—
                            Here corpses
litter a highway's world-line spooling out, a yellow slug-
trail coast to coast, a sun extruded through its year—

29

a lemur's eye, and all it's seen: and what sea's shore
recedes, when night spills out the pupil, brims the orbit
bones and rings out, rainbowed with the slight oil-slick
suggestion of petroleum, of time—the tar pit
retching back its nightmares, so. Earth, too, whose sutures
slip: the San Andreas groans, and in the yawn
of the Great Rift Valley, bones resurface, *click,*
they click like Sherpas scrabbling up the windless scarps
of Kenya, coming up for light—

                For this? Signs: *Searchlight,*
Chloride, Mercury—Skull Mountain, and beyond,
Death Valley, the *Funeral Range, Black Mountains*—

                          Black light licks
this dead exposure, film reversed, as though Lascaux,
mined out with dynamite, were scattered to this scorched
caliche, an umber dust that blows and streaks Camp
Mercury, the road ahead . . . we breathe it, *tic tic,*
still, and feel time pass, feel soft plates coalesce
beneath our fingers, lime laid down in the Cambrian
like the white frost-cap I saw settle on the cloud
that day, when the mushroom lobed, and all the colors
died—

        Oh, that part of the desert is a loose shroud
on the troposphere, a radiance as ambient
as starlight, now. And how the black road flies out
at our feet! How all these nights fly out like shadows,
driven by the red glare of our own birth.
And what's ahead? Night's end, a windshield touched to shards
and sifted into sky again? A sleep? A silence
sliced clean at the closing iris, shuttered
down like a blue garotte across the lens and burst
zero of the instant, here, where the watchface lends
its own light, by the numbers, green and cool, where I first
witnessed—what?—their afterbirth?—their avatar?—
beginnings, say, or ends, rehearsed?—the day they lanced
the surfaces of things, and bled from a fist
of warm earth the quick inhuman light of stars.

*

So sin entered
into things? Dim
orbiter, but
sing! Signal
my position, search
earth's soft cipher's
veer and course,
coordinates' nets torn
or not, nor
instruments' cast
eye askance:

☽
♂
☿

♃
♀
♄

☉

*

Scry thy glass: canst
tell a lost child
more? Nor *whither,* Lord, nor
whence, alas, nor what passed once
for all time
when this chill constellation's
inkling starshine spilled
on lost heaven's o-
oblast?

*

*

O last, sky's lees
in the dish receiver's
shallow goblet: bless
this round echo,
eons dimpled here, pearl
amnion of ancient light, each
apse and nave, each hollow
place pierced, collapsed,
Lascaux, too—O, Sibyl-
lance of far light, fire
light's fiber optic
trick lyre, *sing!*
Signal me which least
implausible of all
Laws last

*

Loss

*

＊

Ssst!
A lucifer's first
pulse struck
on black slate:
lo, *The Universe!*
Now new sunlight's strobe sluice
across an apple's smooth skin:
Adam's? Newton's? Teller's? Tell's?
The just-so story's curvature
unbent from Betelgeuse
to Kells . . .

＊

Which, Abbott?
But choose well!
Recall chaotic mind:
mine: that pitch
and yaw called
sensitivity to first
conditions: such,
a dish receiver's
recapitulation
of the blink initial *O—*
all physics, in a nutshell!—
shot forth—

＊

*

Father
nothing! All that *shalt not*
name God gone: naught how but
chert night pluming nature
as a hand lens
blooms flame—

*

But what can I know,
Father, other
than that the zephyr's
first root's
wrought rain?
is this the West
land's last lay?
Constellation: like
light in a *riddle*—
right, wise man!
Why must this one
have no name?

*

The Encantadas

Where we are is hell

1
Time

T-minus—

           Nothing: *Once upon a time*
my logbook so begins, *in paradise* . . . old fool's-
cap, kept—
           And counting: *10, 9, 8:* the atom's
eve, then, nothing less. *Bang!*—the world began
again, without our knowledge or our help: hell few
enough would witness in its hot actual-
ity; we read it later—*letters, numbers,* some *erratum*
dreamt up out of nothing, bright as bright can be. . . .

Begin, Dear Reader. Conjure Eden, if you will:
the far Pacific, certainly, you'll say, a dream
of cocopalms and bougainvillea, of Paul Gauguin's
soft ochers, orchids, passion flowers, the green
slip of parrots' wings, and stranger fuels,
maybe, flickering the rain forest . . . clear streams
like flowing lenses over young girls' skins
you'll say, limbs flashing into perfect tourmaline
lagoons, the air shimmering with lacewings, dragon-
flies, and oh, the navigator's glass a rose-
window against his eye!
                Forget it. Begin again:
at a quarter-turn around the globe, by no degrees
south latitude, the spyglass goes grisaille.

And how to paint this archipelago? a crow's
wing raked across a rainbow's arc?—words all fit
awkwardly to this, I think. Read Melville *(op. cit.)*—
Darwin—any of the firsthand chronicles; it
always reads the same: volcanic tuff, a scuttle
full of coal in the kaleidoscope, a cullet-
heap of shattered glass and black obsidian
where random DNA slimed out like thready spit
against the rock shore a short time
ago, where seeds and cycad cones and birdlimes
still arrive, by accident, just as we did—

But this anticipates my own odd tale, a bit.
(Anticipates whatever dark wet cellar-
hole we webbed up out of once, what dusty attic
full of blind swooping pterosaurs
we stumble through in sleep, still: what terrors
time alone may hold, whose queer celerities
and halt-steps swept us toward surprise attack—)

⊕

2
Creation

One might as well conceive this story in the cirrose
streamings of volcanic dust across a solar
wind four billion years ago—ground zero,
so to speak, the first shrieking cautery
of earth. One has to start a story someplace; space
would do. The romance of our insularity
is nothing new—
                    But this anticipates,
too. Imagine, then, that gaseous catarrh
all lit like Eniwetok in the white smelter
of the mind's eye, and stirred, turned, tipped
out, vitreous and blazing, so: a scattering
of star-stuff from the far antipodes
of time—
              Iron core and mantle first, the elder
mountain chains and continents, Pangaea's
cracked shell, and then the islands, *ssspink ssspink
ssspink* into the sea. They shone like pan-gold,
bright seeds broad-cast across the Great Arc-Welder's
dream! Well done: with all the sparks and spangles
of His lapidary work still guttering
in place, God smiled, imagined Papeete, Pago-
Pago populous—and knocked his calabash
against his palm six hundred miles off Ecuador,
and turned his face. And what a purgatory
hissed behind his back! An arc of crater-
scraping, cinders, pig-lead slags and smelter ash
all splash into a black square on the Mercator
projection of the mind!
                            It was an Arcady
in broken black and white, a shattered parquet
floor cartographers took centuries to fix.

Or this: imagine rocks rattling like a fist
of birdshot down a coal-chute, say, some baker's
dozen undiscovered moons of Mercury
that funnelled down the wrong end of a Buccaneer's
brass telescope and tore his patch and lodged deep
down some dread dream there amidst the profound breakage
of a dark mind—
                        Sometimes I see it in my own sleep
still, by the lit candelabrum of a Bofors gun: canaries
sputtering the poisoned air in a nightmare's dark
mineshaft, the flickering of yellow flames.
An archipelago. And see again by arc-
light late at night of a thousand cigarettes coughed out
over yet another long, savage, debilitating
siege at chess—
                        But this anticipates the flim-
flam war I mean, in my own good time, to tell about.

$$\oplus$$

3
Codex   Never mind for now what the occasion
was for *chess,* or why it was we billeted
for two years in a cracked glass terrarium
with cactus blooms and mangrove swamps, acacia
trees and guava brush and who knows what too-rare
and ancient sorts of livelihood that lasted where
I'd not been sure we could. We kept the exile's
cage-mentality too long; like monks penned
in the vellum map itself, we xylophoned
tin cups across the ringing iron meridians
from home, and all but went extinct ourselves. We opened
our Pandora's Box and loosed not quite three dozen
extra Furies where such things, already in
magnificent abundance, thrived: *where nightmare-ridden*
margins of this miniature Apocalypse
limned out my orders—cut, as ever, from design—
I kept a book of hours, you'll see, a manuscript
illuminated in the tropical eclipse
of mind that brings out some familiar stars. I've ripped
these pages from that old ephemeris: *the coast*
of Santa Cruz, from where I sit, is like a moonscape
garden (Japanese?)—all rock, rock—

41

                Recall
it, draped in the cracking hides of reptiles, tidal
sumps alive with souls (or so the legend goes)
of once and future murderers dressed out as little
dinosaurs, and set amidst a thick scrawling
of arachnids everywhere like subtitles
rephrasing this one's doubtful move, that one's gross
miscalculation, on and on in a volatile
disgusting prose . . . an Ark whose covenant, in scrolls
of ropy magma scorched and brittle as cicada
shell, read like a map each man held hard, lit
on a flint against his heart—that first, sub-literary
act. Here's memory's white watermark: all
liquifactions come to this: the dessicated
paradise.
                Reduce the sight: the Colloquy
of Ancient Men returns to mind. Terrarium
indeed!—that glass ship shaping West for Faërie,
the year there measuring a hundred on the clock
(classic relativity effect) framed
in the unenchanted realms of men, wherefrom,
repatriated, touching ground, the young seafaring
heroes' spines collapsed: claw fingers raking rheum
in an eye changed, in a world changed, sword
for crozier, what king's son among them saw sacred
text for what it was, or the gray saint's cipher
on the far shore, in the first mist? We've not forseen
him yet, I think; but that's another story, soldered
to the optic nerve where night and the blind spot intersect.
Meanwhile, this tale's titled, say, *Las Islas
Encantadas?* Gods below, say rather *Bali Hai
Recast for Lunatics by the Marquis de Sade,
Combining Elements of South Pacific, Ali
Baba, Sinbad and The Odyssey,*
Or, *How I Wound Up Shipwrecked on a Lee
Shore Live with Lizards, Tortoises and Spiders,
Shellfish, Finches, Not Quite Forty Desperadoes,
and a Single Chess Set . . .*

⊕

4
Zero

Jetsam with a vengeance
that was, too; it almost finished us. Idle
sport! That board became a small parade
ground where each officer could stand his even chance,
on Darwin's terms, against his friends. I have a vision
of the whole thing played out again with cutlasses
and guns—high noon, the hot heart ballasted
with miniballs . . . the men were all too willing
for that kind of thing, I think. If that fine velvet-
lined and inlaid ebony-and-alabaster
box had opened on a matched pair of duelling
pistols, maybe we'd have managed to resolve
its implications faster still. The hell of it
we made was marvelous indeed; but these were lab
conditions, so to speak—or rather labyrinth
conditions: our peculiar struggle for extinction lapsed
into that dark interior parenthesis
behind the brows where insularity begins.
We lost contact. We learned the solipsism
of those islands, so long isolated from each
other that their fauna now can scarcely speak in
common genes, where kindred species drag all slip-
knot strands that trace them to a common beach . . .
cross threads indeed, whose bitter ends we lost,
but one: the chain, so-called, of my command.
We crawl a maze all right, where strange chimeras
gambol black-on-white across a hall of mirrors
in the mind's own compound eye, where Laws
themselves aren't altogether natural, and man
anticipates himself—

As I appear
to do, again. These images recede. Turn
back the clock. Rewind the thread to happier
occasions, prior to this state of nature, tooth
and claw, before we'd lost ourselves in that Plutonic
quadrate cave, and tyranny—our tournament—
began:

$\oplus$

5
The
Truth

Galapagos. The truth is, as it happens,
I served out eternity in World War II
as first lieutenant, USA, with two platoons
of men with murder on their minds and nothing more to
do—at first—than breathe, and paint, chip paint, chip pennies
into endless poker games, and scan the seas
for navies of invading Japanese,
of which there weren't any. It was an easy job
in that respect. If we were in a maze,
it was a simple one, the tic-tac Punnett Square
where swords are crossed and double-crossed. Descartes'
coordinates: you might say we were fixed points, pawns
in the larger context. True, we had no enemies
(in nature); and our outpost was a tiny scar
of dead volcanic tuff without much coast to guard.
But *enemies* . . . Well, *honi soit qui mal y pense,*
as the wisdom goes. *Galapagos.* Our *cause de guerre*
came soon enough—
                              It keeps us all at dagger's
drawn—
                    Do I anticipate? Say once upon
a time such things occurred as held us in suspense
(no other word will do) two years: can I suppose
to trace the chain of circumstance that balkanized
a tiny barracks, broke morale, laid open
dark minds, and brought me to the precipice
I'll get to by and by, to strike a pose *(Peace-*
maker, indeed!) to cheering balconies
of gulls and gooney-birds, to pits of black iguanas,
penguins, crabs, and clapping seals, whose unpacific
theater went up for grabs, as if volcanic
earth had split and I rang down the curtain on its
last catastrophe—
                              Galapagos: a once
and future problem, so: can any compass fix
a man so truly in his life? Coordinates
are difficult to set—

$$\oplus$$

44

6
XYZ

X, Y. To try again:
an ark; an archipelago; Antarctic penguins
strung like clothespins on the line of the equator
wing to wing with tropical flamingoes, frigate-
birds, pelagic albatrosses riding winds
above the flightless cormorants and coastal waders
here, Hawaiian petrels, African egrets . . .
all compass points are brought to zero here. *Forget,*
forget, this is the logic of the tame herons,
rails and shearwaters, the terns and flycatchers
that made their passage once, that took this plunge
for all time, never to return—

        Rooks errant,
so to speak. I wrote: *Such ligatures*
as bind us to our home shores stretch; here, in this
strange projection, latitudes and longitudes
distort, like lines in the rope-net hammock where off-duty
gunners lounge and read their mail and write their cheerless
letters home—
    I knew; I was a student
of their mail. It was my job to censor
it. For what?—to keep the garrison from leaking
certain secrets kept safe on these islands since
the Pliocene. Eyes only lizards here: *Stewed*
meat tonight please write PS whats new sincerely
yours Dear Dad good weather here (ten thousand leagues
under the sun what's new) *signed your fond son's*
turned twenty-one today my razor's turned
up missing hope he cuts himself God damn him trained
the guns on flyspecks on the clouds what ducks
hawks hawk-moths gulls bats dragonflies the local Wing
Commander's ass—
    And there it was: what doctor
of these less-than-humane letters could have missed
the change in tone in time, the strain?— no mystery
about it: *do what here / don't do / damned nothing doing*
here these days . . . How could I hope to interdict
the thoughts I saw developing—with pruning scissors?
Cut the story short? Well, no. That text restores
itself, I think, in ways no man predicts
or properly recalls. Cut lines come back like echoes
in an empty cave, where Baltra's migratory

45

bats passed through four long decades ago . . .
the vacancy resounds—*Hope everyone's O K
at home* . . . These thoughts deflect off rock, to locate
us in space, in time, *P S X X O O*—
Coordinates: life signals its position so.

$$\oplus$$

**7
Log-
book**

Begin again. *Postmark Baltra, A K A
South Seymour (all the islands have two names here)* circa
1942:

*Review: two companies of Puerto
Rican infantry. One fixed-gun shore
emplacement old enough to have repulsed the Ark.
One J-Boat. Bomber squadron. Airstrip. Scarecrow
antiaircraft battery—*
That's all, or
all we brought; though all day long unfriendly ack-
ack echoed back at us from the bills of a land-based air corps
less exotic than our own. The slings and arrows
of this island's very life: *today mistook
high-soaring albatross for some poor windblown Zero
wafted here from Asia, half a world off course . . .
I tracked it with the Bofors gun, while oystercatchers
taxied far below, and seagulls stooped like stukas
on the shingle, screaming, hatching clam-
ware on the rocks, to shrapnel . . . nacreous
shell-casings everywhere, all calibers, great caches
of them, live and dead: red crabs and blue crustaceans,
carapaces (olive drab) where columns
of reptilian armor once churned sand across
the desert highlands . . . shells remain, like turrets
bleaching in the sun, their antique battle stations
manned by geckos and tarantulas—against
what steep odds? By night, the green sea-turtles
mine the strand a hundred eggs at once,
while on the beachheads black marine iguanas
carry out amphibious maneuvers
like the leathernecks they are. We never
fraternize. I watch the great man-of-war
birds gliding overhead, and think of terrapins*

that once took wing. We walk, like sandpipers or gulls.
We've got our own beachcombing operations,
picking slowly over rocks, staring
through the still, warm tidepools of this finisterre,
this end-of-land—for what? For oracles,
for signs of war, or peace, of unknown perishing
armies . . . all the evidence I've ever had
was fishing floats. (Glass spheres—I'd found a nest
of them, net-slimed, and shimmering—)

                                        Oh, I recall
deep *ennui,* days passing one into the next,
the moon a beat of moth-wings overhead,
and sun to sun unchanging, a swarm of red bees
in memory—
                We've heard the artificial breeze
inside the seashell like a line gone dead.

⊕

8
Hours

Time flows one way, it's said; *there are no traces*
of the future. Past is past. But who can tell?
If I lift up these desktop souvenirs,
my old glass fishing floats, and turn and candle
them against the sun, why, tortoises
appear again—ridiculous, distorted
green shapes, changing—
                        Copulating, roger, wilco,
wilco, roger, all day long—
                        The heavy dance
of life a zillion years ago. What evidence
had we for anything on earth? A whelk,
a winejar held against the ear; the fine quill-
work of gulls against the sky's palm; black
sand beaches sucked to sea and then washed back
again each season, passing through the glass iris
of the eye like night—
                Erase
the record, then. This was a timeless place.
We blinked across the dark cracked carapace
of Baltra to the other bits of spalled
stone offshore, to Albemarle, and Santa Cruz
and James. If there were any message in this broken

bottle of an archipelago, the ghost crabs,
lava crabs and Sally-lightfoots spelled
it out: *escape; hide; die.* The buccaneers'
rude X's scuttling sideways. Red runes
gone at a footstep. Disappearing ink.

⊕

9
Disap-
pearing

Well, that was in the nature of the Encantadas
too, I think. Through history, they've rinsed
back in and out of view. The unclear data
of the early navigators indicate
two archipelagoes in close proximity, laced
flat across the zone of the equator
like a pair of painted sea-snakes illustrating
some old globe, a burned half-braid of licorice
extruded round its own black shadow, doubling space,
where time, too, observed some marvellous
reverse. Inertial frames perplex. Were these two separate
lines of islands, or a single eyelash-lick,
a cinder, a disturbance of the vellum
in the navigator's eye? I recognized this spirit
in the place, loose and indeterminate: Melville's
awful lilypads of dead silicic ash,
basaltic spines, high bluffs and veldts and vitrified
black sand two centuries observed to drift
across the charts, unfixed—
                                        This wandering
was over with for good, of course, when Darwin
made his landfall here. The year mankind began
again: 1835: the *Beagle*
found the archipelago in place, and fixed
it there forever, spindled on a small bird's beak.
What change! Of course, the world's been brought to focus
since. Each small astigmatism on the surface
of the sea is marked, each shoal, each benthic peak
has been imagined to the second of an arc
by now; no man an island but he's known,
discovered *here* in the satellite's offical survey—

Shown here backlit once for all, against the gnomon
of a cesium atomic clock, an awkward

48

radioactive shadow cast down amongst
the birds and other changing dinosaurs and monk-
faced, mole-sized Miocene homunculi,
who, gazing out the black ports of the pupils
even now anticipate the stars.

⊕

10
Clocks

Oh, and the pulse
of tides, and trace-lines of the great migrating
whales, transcontinental flights of humming-
birds, the neap and flow of continents
themselves across the planet's shell. All clocks. All tinsel
on a time-lapse photographic plate—

My pulse rate
may have changed as well; although the transit
of the sun was visible, and stars condensed
against my glasses every night, a citrine
light leaked underneath the eyelids every dawn,
and every dawn we woke into the same trance.
What change could we detect? If life lingered on
here longer than in other places, I'd call *boredom*
to account—for tortoises' longevity,
for relict lichens, lizards, insects held on pins
and needles here—ours was a very pure suspense.
Except, of course, our lives across the *board.*
Here alone the sandglass turned on time, and chivvied
every man to move, or forfeit. This was martial
law we lived by. Endgame stopped the clock, and fixed
the pieces in position in the mind until next
time. Mistakes! These islands on the sea themselves,
a still array of specimens, sharp shells
of beetles, pinned and shimmering like flaws
in the lightly silvered mirror man observes his image
in—

Unnatural philosophy! So much
for Time. If continents had drifted off their shelves
to smithereens across a nearby ocean's floor
we never would have noticed it. We lived like djinn
in a killing jar, exacting vengeance each on each.
No glimpses left us less forlorn. No distant engines
troubled us. Who saw the roseate fluorescence

49

of the wider war at all? We held a niche
no wider than the game, while finches' genes
outside presumably kept calculating chance
mutations two by two like inchworms on the Ark
(as who knows what DT's still dancing paradiddle
down the desperate dreams of the Joint Chiefs?)—
if paradise was changing all around us, chess
was more immediate. We made our moves. If arcane
knots were being cut, and Darwin's riddle-
of-the-finch undone on the same sword's edge, if
Cain's own chromosomes would bear the marks etched
in imagination by some red radium-
painted second hand advancing like a lancet
in the dark of the dark night we managed to achieve
our victory, what could we know of that? V J
would be the least of it. If acetylene
flames played twice across the Great Chain
while we were fast asleep—

                    What change! and what man dreamt
it? *M*, and its equivalents, and us—as if
this light just reaching us—

                    Alas, blown Ilium
alight behind us, us halfway returned to swine.

$$\oplus$$

11
Orders
    However that may be—whatever new unholy
marvels might soon shroud the west Pacific
in a red cocoon (and who knows what sweet moly
may preserve our children now)—my own assignment
didn't require an Einstein. Try to stay alert;
that's all. A queer, inverse Calypso's spell, specific
I suppose to every dead-end military
outpost, was the problem here. In point of fact
my orders as the Battery Commander
were to keep the ninety-millimeter
(Bofors) antiaircraft guns maintained and manned
and set to fire on ninety seconds notice. No matter
that the nearest hostile planes were out of range on
shipboard somewhere west of Yap or Guam or Truk and
no alert would ever come:
                    I've reckoned

our position due east of that origin
in mid-Pacific where the Dateline cuts the Line,
and calculated any airborne mission reaching
east for Baltra from the Carolines
will have to leap eight thousand miles of ridge
and trench and open ocean, penetrating
six hours deep into the day before—

⊕

12
Analog

Tomorrow and tomorrow's sun declined along
its sine-wave, porpoising between the tropics,
summer, winter, equinox. It tacked the trade
winds both ways, and I traced its path. The Bofors
gun was fitted with a crude analog
computer: two men tracked a target optically,
one estimated range; the black box *tic-tocked*
out coordinates. We practiced on the Air Force
once a month or so. With any luck
we punched our cufflinks through the trailing target
sleeves; that's practice. But if discipline decayed
as aim improved, was I surprised to get
the pilot's angry call? Beside himself he swore
one of my gun crews grazed him, shots
shrieking underneath his lumbering Dakota's
belly—
　　　　Wide miss my ass the son-of-a-bitches
were tracking me the whole way what kind of warped
son of a whore—
　　　　　　　　　And so forth. What could I say? Should
I have said the men were bored? They were. I coo'd
and clucked until the poor clipped clay pigeon's
feathers smoothed. Of course the men knew all the warplanes'
silhouettes by heart. The subtleties of engine-
cowlings, tailplanes, wingforms, from any angle, pitch
and yaw and roll—Darwin never knew his finches
better than these gunners, theirs. Say enemy
or friend, say which is which? *Dakota—Zero—Zeke—*
all this peculiar rote taxonomy
was printed on the face of special-issue Bicycle
cards. Days I watched their solitaire, while seagulls'
shadows played across the game—
　　　　　　　　　　　　　The nearest

51

hostile target, where? The men flash cards and nurse
the vision of these shapes they'll never see, except
in silhouette . . . I watch them squat down, strike spades
off the side of the deck for hours on end in a septic
frame of mind, like speechless aborigines
absorbed in the manufacture of the first blades
on earth, chert flakes, the first hand-work, like butchery
in mind—

       My orders read *prepare for imminent*
assault: four of eight guns firing on a minute-
and-a-half's alert. Consider what it meant!
a short leash to the guns, day in, day out! The beach
was out of range. Two hundred yards away was *hors-de-*
combat. Two hundred centuries, a minute more or
less in geologic time. . . .
              These orders
guaranteed the landscape in the hand-held mirror
was the only place a man on watch could stray, and there
lay danger. Who could say what distant nightmares
might in the dark of any night wash overboard
and drift to us, what sights might climb the red-rimmed eye-ledge
any dawn? Here anything seemed possible:
the topsails of the Beagle, or the gelid
crest of some disgusting Ordovician
man-of-war hove in offshore from what hot pisspool
ocean, long gone—why not? Two years in that corridor
of orange sunrises we raised up swollen lids
below a low salute to one blurred vision,
the round *rising sun,* the artificial
sun hung limp as laundry on the radar
mast of some Imperial flagship Yamamoto
never showed us—

⊕

13
Geodesy

                                    Though I think I felt
it, heavy in the center of the wide chart's
web, waiting, belly full of folded
wings: phantom carrier: a mote
unfixed in the shifting humors of mirage.
We scried the gunsight for a sheaf of shadows, shards
of night passed back and forth from eye to heart to fist
again, feathering the empty margins
of imagination like a gnomon's
black blade in mind, where artifice
begins: here was a blueprint of the ocean, shored
up in a shallow stone basin, the magus'
dark reflecting pool where memory and omen
merge, concentric wavelets overlap, Omega
matches Alpha, light itself foreshortens
on a star's point—
                                    And by these points the No-Man
navigates, and here his art: the maker's
plain-weave lines laid over water like a weir
to hold his continents and islands hard, and net
the sun's reflection fast in place, and hold the very
oceans still—until its basin's bones unknit,
and all this small creation seeps away.

                                                        Aware
of nothing underneath the round calvarium
of heaven but ourselves, what can we know? Innate
geography? The realms of sleep? See, the minute
hand set turning on a turning hour
hand is our vernier, and focusses the lens.
We calibrate these intervals by parallax,
by memory and foresight—
                                    So, the mind relaxes
into sleep, the way the nacreous
reflection of the full moon loses line, lanced
open on a piling, say: imperfect pearl
to mother-of-pearl, the light seeps out across
the surface of the sea—
                                    And this is the white at the world's
end, the empty parchment map. If calipers,
set hard, stab through this parchment now and then, we twirl

them slowly, so, and feel strange sea-worms writhe like bait
beneath the surface of the dream—

A Cyclops'

ruined dream—

⊕

**14
Scry-
ing**

        Thus telescopes collapse
the sky, and consciousness whorls up that blank abyss
where no man's origins anticipate
his end—as though this were some clear abscissa
lancing through the map into a lapse
of light where even the best glass eyes go black.

                            Again:
forget the war, forget how past and futures braid
together in a conscious mind. Call this Calypso's
sweet breath, blown through a conch-shell, held in a green
glass bubble in my hand. *This is a fishing
float,* I wrote. *Japan? The round curve is marred
where a blowpipe once whirled loose. I think about cool lips,
I think about my wife, my family. A married
man. Alas for whom? A small green artificial
world held upside down in hand*—deciphered
later, maybe, dropped to some apocalypse. . . .
*A paper-weight. Imagine, fishbowl farmhouse, myriad
reflective snowflakes settling down a liquid breeze,
as though deep down the ephemerides
some small essential zero's burst, the sun's collapsed,
design's undone*—

              And so these islands seemed. I'll read
the rest: *Sometimes this seems the terrible
simplicity, the formlessness of new creation.
Earth-at-seed. Sometimes it seems the rubble
at the end of industry, the font
thrown down and melted down, the green creche
crushed*—

        Unhealthy humors of mirage.
What change? We kept our watch by night, and fanned

54

ourselves by day in the bright shade of the acacia
trees, embracing calenture, the gemmary
of broad ocean blinding us. I felt what merge
of memory and expectation ricochetted
like sea-light on the caged eyes of Daedalus
himself, the handy-man himself, whose art
reminded me of this. The wreckage, shards,
the well-made thing reduced, destroyed. Dead loss.

⊕

**15
Terra
Incog-
nita**

Ah, *industry*—the cog-wheel bull coiled turn by turn
into the perfect epicenter of the china-
shop: I saw the whole spool reversed
again, old mountain chains unbuilt, all Quaternary
time tossed back, its careful joineries
undone, its fine distinctions smelted down. The rivers
of volcanic rock suggested this, and the loose
screes strewn everywhere like bits of terracotta
scattered when the last leaf-mold broke: *dead genera,*
I wrote, *the last ghost guttered out. No referents
for Life left, no fossicking for cold clues
among such cracked thoughts*—

                     This was the cautery
of life itself on earth I saw, an earth left empty
as we'd leave our own dead nest, in the event.
But never mind for now what *terra incognita*
that became, in time, what creatures have or haven't
followed this trajectory before in umpteen
centuries, their arc traced out in cogs and needle
gears in God's dark gunsights, say—
                     Who knows what damned
detrital wilderness we'll all have willed of heaven
in the end? *Descent:* my tale is Humpty-Dumpty,
with Miltonic overtones: what chivalry
could hope to reassemble it?
                     I played my own king's
horses warily. I told the moons like worry
stones: each whirling, finger-polished piece God shovelled
down his clear ecliptic reliquary
overhead, I followed with the gunsight, linking

it to earth, thus: moon-shot, star-shot, sun-shot,
tic tic tic, computer plotting elevation,
range and azimuth by automatic clockworks,
faithful, accurate, a strange half-sentient
thing. Why not? Perhaps it held a vision
of the whole zodiac in mind, all quarks
and constellations wheeling on their axes
in the dark inside a small black box where
every possible trajectory exists
by cool mechanical analogy.
                              Descent
he said. O, luck! like Alice through the bisqueware
chip, we've crossed our glass. What man in nineteen forty-
two could have predicted *that* queer antecedent
to the gunsight? Microchip: the square
projection of the crystal ball—imagine, 4-D
programmatic greenhouse! Earth-at-seed,
and re-evolving seas and lands, to frame all Eden
in a pane of sand—

⊕

**16
Future**   This is the conjury
of engineers, the djinni-in-the-jar
at last—*that's* artifice!—the ancient mirror held
to nature held against the mind of man! Imagine,
star-ship earth careened and rigged, half-modelled
mathematically and corked and bottled,
all in hand: a green and changing message in
machine code, *zero, one*—that analogue which apes
intelligence, anticipates all change, the home-
world's subtle futures each revealed by orbital
concatenations, turns, the pole-star's wanderings
above, tectonic drifts deep down the shell . . . what shapes
us, in between, in middle earth, where genus *Homo,*
treed and gibbering, once took the corsair's
way to shape an arc for some wide yonder
out of Africa? Can we forecast that course,
compute that final end, according to the cross-hairs
in a clear mind's lens?
                              This is geodesy,

or magic, then——the careful stringing of the gourd
whose smooth green surface is a sounding board
held close against the heart of man: imagine
that original marine-corps odyssey,
those oddball sub-men with their awful sub-machines,
their island-hopping conquest of the world! The clue
lies in the conch-shell, listen: *Homo habilis*
at work, whose handblown future in a dizzy
whiff of ozone comes to seem like some ballistics
exercise gone wrong, like some concluded
tale involving an obsidian-
and-milk-glass chessboard, chimpanzee, and stoneaxe
hammer——
        Homo sapiens, oh, my! Absurd
computer chessboard re-projecting Adam
in the garden here, who plays his planet
more like pinball, hard, *ding, ding*——until an onyx
particle arcs out, arachnid trace, a fine silk
trail——to *impact,* so: entire anatomies
of software spilling loose, a scree of silicon,
ceramic insulators, shivered glass, eight-legged
random and imaginary numbers sewed
inside the program's network now unknit
and loose across the earth . . . the whole silly
post-apocalyptic picture like a black egg
in the sand, unhatched. An episode
unread. As yet.

⊕

**17
History**
        But why anticipate? Erase
this Future—foolish tale—begin again,
with History: an open book, a parrot's
perfect memory, who always cites his source.
For example: *In Farragut's day, straight razors
were forbidden to the seamen. A ship's barber
worked full-time . . .*
        And I know why. *Our* operatic
follies never came to blood; although a grave
on James bore witness to the possibilities:
*A duel at daybreak, 1813, quiet harbor
ringing with the third discharge, the pistol bullet*

drifting through a young lieutenant's breast . . . It gave
me pause, that tale. If I felt ill at ease
commanding here, why not? What books I may have kept
inside a seabag by my bed I took an
education from—and earned my captaincy
before I left, which shows what History can do,
whispering across the years like some wise toucan
bright as muzzle-flash against a pirate's
ear, echo chamber where a gun's report
repeats, repeats: I learned hard lessons out of Porter's
logs, Morrell's and Darwin's, Dampier's—

Dampier: raptor

of the Spanish Main . . . Recall him to his quarter-
deck, calipers in hand, his charts,
his glass, his cross-shelf sextant, his gracious Queen's
letters of marque. . . . Deep in the hold live tortoises
(his larder) crawl across twelve tons of quince
marmalade he's captured from the Spanish, tart
garnish for a cruise already gorged
on bullion—

Or Morrell: *see embers trace*
above his head when Narborough blows into sequins
here, a hundred years ago. His sealer Tartar's
seams ooze pitch and tar runs off her rigging, scorched
sails scarcely twitching in the windless dark.

Suspense is what recalls this pyrotechnic
tale, I think: we wait, we watch the decks
warp up, the sailors wet and wet again the kerchiefs
clenched against their breath like hot red gills, and the reefs
of floating pumice bobbing in the slow simmer
of the harbor, the ship itself a brown sphinx moth
perched on a roaring lantern's rim—

⊕

**18
Set
Pieces**

I fixed

such points in history in mind (with some surmise)
and tried to plot the sequence of the myth.
Sometimes I hold the fishing float just so,

in hand, and peer inside as though the Spanish plate
fleet plied the sea-lanes from Manila to the Isthmus,
preyed upon by Buccaneers again—as though
our fate were tied up with the Fate of Nations, played
out here below our very guns again . . . .

    I spun the glass to fix the azimuth
of various events. In time how many desperate
captains anchored here and put ashore for *agua,*
huevos, and *galapagos?*—a ghostly
history indeed, a roll of all the spirits
(legend says) who still remained here, reincarnate
in a darker shape: *Call that iguana*
there *Tupac Yupanqui, Tenth Inca,*
Cusco prince who set sail from the coast
at Guayaquil with a vast fleet of balsa rafts,
to find this archipelago before Cortez cast
shadow on the sea . . . Call that iguana
over there *Fray Tomas de Berlanga,*
Third Bishop of Panama, who drifted
off course eight days on a dead helm on a blank
chart before he made landfall on Santa Fe . . .

    This is 1535. The Beagle's *anchor*
chain rings out in Wreck Bay in just
three centuries, to bring St. Francis of the Finches,
Charles Darwin, my second Bishop, manque.
Call that *green heron by the shore Kamehameha's*
Queen, and mine; Their Majesties are homeward bound
one hundred ninety-eight days out of London
for Oahu, dead of measles, under
escort of the seventh Lord Byron, aboard the Blonde.

    As for other pieces, choose yourself,
from the ranks and files of this benighted rookery
replete with dead seadogs and cutthroats, silver
thieves and brave heroes, whalers and rakes and ragged
castaways and God's own odds and ends, and us:
for knights, choose Dampier (I've suggested), or Morrell,
or David Porter, Alexander Selkirk (Crusoe),
Lord Vancouver—no, choose David Farragut,

midshipman, serving Porter in these Encantadas,
destined to become the first full Admiral,
U S N, one day. *He took a prize crew*
aboard a British whaler captured by the frigate
Essex, *here; it was his first command. His rapier*
must have dragged the deck behind him like a seabird's
tail—Mr. Farragut was twelve years old.

At twice
that, twenty-six when I arrived, I was the greybeard
of the battery, the sage, the wisest
head on Baltra, doubtless. Twenty-six was
Darwin's age.

$$\oplus$$

**19
Island
Life**

Descent: *Island life kills*
flight. Fact. So one by one our quills
fall to the parchment; verse by numbered verse
is History, while God writes Life Himself
in serifs deep inside the cell, where elvers
coil and intertwine through time and trace
the complex branchings of the branching trees . . .
transcriptions inked in minuscule in the one language
Darwin lacked to crack the mysteries
of *change.* (Would we pass on the traits that *we* acquired
in those two years? I wondered.) Caught between Lamarck
and Mendel, Darwin never understood the links which
formed his chain—and still he guessed why all the awkward
kiwis, emus, cassowaries, auks,
moas, dodos, rails, ducks, *lost flight—*

What Arks
of queer unwary avifauna once relinquished
wind, and never won it back! What change!
On islands, where no breeze blows inshore, offshore winds wash
feathers out to sea. Survivors walk. Less risk—
and we, too, left alone too long to languish
in an island aviary all too strange
and rich with obsolescent forms and odd grotesques
of every shape and texture, giants, dwarves—
what change could we expect? *Surprise attack?*
A note in a furry bottle? *Fact: exotic taxa*

threaten island life. I know, I've seen the Orphic
text, four letters in a brine slurry, cursive
lines leading back—I've seen the serifs
atrophy before my eyes, I've felt the wharf-
rat scurry through my dreams, to swim, to cross the surf-
line, littering the beach with strange tracks. . . .

⊕

20
Surprise
Attack

Survive,
my inmost orders must have read; yet who protects
us from ourselves, when orders overlap? I felt huge
shadows glide across Oahu, droning, karmic
interweavings, wings across the earth—
and wrote: *sometimes I watch our bombers practice, taxi*
up the tiny airstrip, stop, and turn, and whooosh
rush back, bombracks scarcely clearing hot tarmac—
and often then the heat mirage appears to wreathe
the image, withering and softening an airfoil's
fine leading edge, until the whole squadron
shimmers helpless in the sun, squab
and earthbound as the rest of us . . .
                              Then feral
pigs and tortoises would stalk my mind, extinct
creatures, all creatures doomed and apterous
and changed—*and what may after all come after us?*
As Darwin wrote, *we may infer what havoc any*
new beast of prey must cause before the instincts
of indigenous inhabitants become adapted
to the stranger's craft or power . . .

                              The tyranny
we suffered was peculiar, and I doubt for all
his vatic gifts that even Darwin's prophesies
could have accounted for the awful circumstances
here: we were a small world: six officers,
a concrete barracks twelve by twenty-four, the feral
game—
          That came here, I suppose, the way berserkers
would, the way the fierce wild pigs once did, by ship.
Imagine this: a fateful landfall here, off Circe's
dark coast, the lowering away in jolly-

boats, surf breaking over feathered oars, the bishop's
incantations, keelson's crunch on rock . . . and rook
and knight and king and queen and sixteen pawns awash
in two waves, black and white. Like Yap or Kwajelein
or Ponape we suffered our assault. I watched
the whole thing happen, too—our miserable rogue's
roost wrested from my loose grip, to—

                                   Misrule,
interregnum, call it: our poor frail ecology
collapsed—at what? that courtly pressure, parlor
sport, without the firing, as they say, of a single
shot.

$$\oplus$$

**21
Tourna-
ment**

    It took time, of course. This was a visceral
assault, requiring anger, which grew like cultured pearl
inside us as the days passed by. The seagulls
swung like true carrion birds above. We played
the tournament together, but we planned
our strategies alone. This was a perilous
siege—this was a black and white waste land
where each man wheeled his artificial legions
counter to humane intelligence,
until, in two short months, this curse had fanned
the men through monomania and murderous
and sullen competition to a pitch
you'd not believe was possible. Immured
in the mind's own deep sulphurous red calderas
where we'd made our beds and slept, capitulation
was a commonplace all day, each day—*mate—check-
mate, check—*

          We changed: devolved: a Jekyll-
Hyde phenomenon. Was this *extreme duress?*
I watched that jackass brio GI's substitute for logical
reflection in their lives leach out—replaced
by what, a cool reptilian languor alternating
with some kind of beady hot jihad
mentality I'd never seen before, reserved
for nothing in the world but *chess.* The altar
each man let some blood on, then; each had

his turn. The game revolved, as regular as surf
breaking in the inner ear. The afterimage
of that checkered board would burn all night, and each
man lying silent, and each wrong move a match-
light curling like an eyelid over his
insomnia . . .
                    Then dawn, another day to go,
lose or win—each dawn the whole damned intrigue
again: the quick cross-stitch of glances through the hiss
of hot water in the shaving mirrors—
pantheon of officers in heavy stucco
masks, each safety razor balanced on a blood-streaked
chin: we made a terrifying frieze, morose
and stupid gods at toilet, say—hysteric
chorus reenacting rosy-fingered sunrise:
cirrus feathers off the sink like lifting mist,
and red sun open in a lidless stare
above a nicked blue-blade horizon, half immersed
and foamy with the spindrift—Lord, our own blank eyes
on one another, sidelong, saurian,
the whole place hissing like a nest of copperheads.
Comrades-at-arms; well, we were that. It had to stop.

$$\oplus$$

22
Excur-
sion

Just here, I'd calculate, in the normal course of the story-
teller's art, by etiquette (Copernican,
to think of it), there ought to come *the gruesome
part.* I've set my stage for murder, no? But the best
that I'll deliver's this: a struggle, let's say witnessed
by one Icarus of us who flew the coop,
who took the J-Boat prize, and sailed to Santa Cruz.
Excursion rates, he writes . . . *the pterodactyls nested
in the high scrub woods, I guess—an unprotected
place. Too bad; I found their eggs all over, antique
teapots rooted up and trampled in the roost.
Wild pigs do this. I picked around awhile, and noticed
where one shallow mound in the light soil lay intact
and undisturbed. Inside, two eggs, unbroken,
round, white, three fingers wide maybe—I raised
one up against a match and blew the dust*

away, and maybe I imagined the baroque
little creature hanging just off-center in the yolk sac,
tiny gargoyle, beak curved down, huge eyes—

                                                    Then Jesus
suddenly this awful bellowing, no distance
up the slope, I heard this bellowing, the jaws
of Death, I thought, the whole prehistoric sty
of fucking dinosaurs exhumed at once—I tossed
the egg (that's us), ran into the trees to try
to get a closer look, and did—one hopeless tortoise
looking old as earth herself was stumping towards
me, chugging forward fast, while a great wild sow was dragging
back with all her might and shaking, wrenching, side
to side like some immense rat-terrier,
jaws clamped fast to the rim of the carapace. A piece tore
loose, and the reptile lurched ahead a moment, dragon's
neck extended, frantic, torn, trying to hide—
never a chance. The pig closed in again,
and the whole scene over again—again—I can't recount
the rest; I left. God knows it looked like agony.
They eat them in the end, I'm told. I shied a sharp rock
hard, and ran like hell—

                    Las Islas Encantadas,
thus, *like hell, like hell, like hell.* I'd shrugged
it off myself, easily enough: I broke
the egg without a thought. Well, what taught us
this would see us home again somehow,
I hoped. But the vision's stayed with me. The shock
of nations greeting one another here on
earth: the grunting tortoise, the feral sow.
Recall long afternoons punctuated
with rifle fire from infantry recruits
without a thought in mind; a crumpled heron,
twitching on the tidal flat; a gunshot seal.
Nothing in the world to do but wait.
By the time the war was over and the last crew-
cut killer of us had shipped off Isla
Baltra Stateside, there was no biology
to speak of left, apart from insects, and pelagic
birds that still, despite us all, stopped by.

One showed me what to do.
                    Today I watched him wheel
and spiral over the island's high eastern ledge,
where Baltra falls away a hundred feet, furl
his great wings, stall, swoop fast and tip
a booby sideways, spill its meal . . . the piracy
of frigate-birds, who steal their fish mid-flight. Fateful
omens. I'll offer him what he can catch, soon
enough—

⊕

**23
Flight**

                    And who anticipates? antipodes
of sea or sky, of black on white, the iris
of the evening opening again, or full moon, opposite.
I struck an attitude. I watched both globes eclipse
part way behind the far horizon's rim, like turbid
glass losing line, softening the way a rose
window might soften in a great cathedral
fire the moment just before its last collapse:
and spun between them, the bird, a high, torpid
wheeling, wheeling on the thermal breeze
that braids up from the vortices of dead calderas,
curling, wing-lit, white flame on a lampwick.
Far below, the ocean, eddying, disturbed
and viscid, stirred the center of my own orbit
bones, horizonless, where aqueous
reflections of the stars slide out like quicklime
on the night, and continents still queasy
in their beds lie by my leave, unsutured
as this tale:
                    There's no release to this, I tell
you!—you wishing for a murder, Reader!—war crimes!
worse!—me wasting words like *eyeglass goes grisaille,*
gone west, etc., steeped in nonesuch
science, or its high-church eschatology . . . .

What change? What change can I recall, or work?
I'm doomed to overstatement, last as first:
a sun's reintroduction, new forms of worship, fustian
as ever: *air, earth, water, fire—*

65

Fire: Japan, behind a jagged line of craters
west of Narborough and Albemarle, was washed
in a new radiance; and sleepy Washington
was somewhere on the other side of Ecuador,
where the moon rose off its long silver stem; I watched
it wavering. And where was I? On a rock bluff
a hundred feet above the sea a quarter
way around the measured earth, the summer solstice
somewhere to my right, midwinter to my left
somewhere, where the polestar nightly doused itself, a soul
at its extremity dissolving in the bleary oxides
of a hazy sunset on a bad evening on the shortest
day of the year, let's say, *tic toc* . . . .

                                        Hostilities
would have to cease soon, I knew, although the warhawks
I'd be facing in the morning with an awkward
alibi might not agree. Still, I was sure,
the lens that focussed us was burning us, and my forced
ending, ludicrous as this long affadavit
sounds, was quick: I chucked the little chessmen one by one off
the world's edge. Splash, splash: pennies in the well, worn facets
flashing. It was a made wish, without remainder: divide,
conquer.
        Now, Dear Reader, hold the still-whole, gravid
atom of the green glass fishing float some steadfast
first lieutenant turned captain turned father
once upon a time brought home, to scry his own fear
or his own youth through, maybe, the told days spherical,
cool, smooth as ivory chessmen ticking past
the palm. You'll read a real story there.
A man might dream this, badly. A sorcerer
might hold this, as they do, as though it were a caul,
vitreous around the earth and the green sky,
and see suspended there a knight, a tiny seahorse
embryo, fixed for good in the mind's eye.

*

Mind minted *thee,*
old dah-dit,
encantada'd orbiter, O,
antedated Ike dime
turned, re-
turned again
against the sky's
flecked velvet—
but reflect: echolocate
x, y, z: The End.
Send, child,
that I may receive

*

Nor *Constellation Siva,*
yet?—still, *constellation,*
nonetheless: the last half-
century's sure reason writ
on God's grid like pitch-
blende blinking in its seine?
One cinder's hot sensation,
surely, Lord; but the second's
counting, and the third's
thought: cross hatch its matrices:
see yourself what pure mind's
wrought:

*

*

Why, nothing, then,
but that blue cathode,
God's thought!
Thyrse and dithyramb,
or RAM wraith,
thus?—
the first one's
wood wand's
poppy-bloom on blank slate,
bang!
The Universe,
etc.—

*

Resoldered in the sandglass, here:
where old lights' world-lines
lyse and nick and reanneal,
a noctilucent ampersand's
sine cut, in *Anno* nil,
in memory:
where searchlights strake
the chalkboard night,
where No-Man's works
redress his days,
we're all erased
for lack of words,
where every star's
recalled the same
recalled the same
and now a new sun rises like
an embolism to the brain

*

70

*

O send some sun
sign, high
pyromancer, morse
oracle, cool Navigator-
by-the-dots! Dead
reckon by the red key,
God damned, touched
and counting: *datum*,
datum, digitized fire
drowned in the compound
of the sky's spalled
ought—

*

Solve sky thy-
self, Father,
etherless:
thy lucifer's
first sulphur fire, salt
sea, or ground:
is this the *nth*
root of the Great
Tree, all gods', girt
green again, in Sol's cirque
drowsing?
Count down:

*

*

Orbiter, O, better
half and second sight, sixth
sense, thou ground lens
and tortoise shell
of a sound, if artificial
intelligence—
send

*

Then
mind-
made
heaven
zigs
fire
forth for
thee,
true
One?—

*

72

Typhoon

The wisdom of his country had pronounced by means of an Act of Parliament that before he could be considered as fit to take charge of a ship he should be able to answer certain simple questions on the subject of circular storms.

20 December: Gypsy to Aztec we picked up survivors at 14 27 - 12807 five officers and thirty-six men.

Rule y against your chart, Dear Reader: broken *X-miss* signalled over time, the year the old mechanics cracked, its V J-tailed, to riddle us: as neither *whither, Fool,* nor *whence,* nor *what hope you on earth this little while—*

Why, then, the question: posed like the crescent moon above the masthead, dotted with a guest star, let's say, bright in daytime—

0940 Gr & Gyp V Leop ack last sig out

Date-line-like, itself, in point of fact, as wasn't that the real news? *Space-time,* for God's sake?—all past-time's tight curve's jack-in-the-pulpit boxed [T Y X Z] and no more circle squared: the first, dim, tempest-eyed instant's snowy contrail struck sunwise through a sea's horizon, sunk and rising—

goodluck affirmative out

Quantum chromosome of future time?—Typhoon tracked off a Navy chart like some lost joke Poseidon upchucked, punctuating heaven in that damned, last, exclamatory way—

1000 S3 V Raven I have to lie in this vicinity

This story bears west too, by due south, abscissal to that mid-Pacific origin we'll mark, say, by the old penultimate, ψ, drawn so, like upsilon lanced, or a bent gunsight,

1115 Rav V Hall I cannot pickup any E of u give me B & R 090 4000 yds ship keep clear iden yourself

or Neptune's snapped fish spear? No, rather, arc and barrel of its brass half-$\varnothing$, call this an instrument: my sextant, set above the navigable semi-circle of this story, so to speak, the smooth bore of its telescope a sanity by which the awful starfire over us might still, by some sweet sight-reduction, come back to its burial at sea.

Ssst, asterisk: I think of that dead watch
through numberless years to come, and truly I wonder—
not *why*, quite—

*S V Q did
u rec last
miss*

                    But why anticipate? Sidereal
considerations got us to this fix, Dear
Reader. You know how it all comes out: *We won.*
The End. And there's a fine beginning, star drill
on stone—straight to the point, for once,
the period I'm writing in, its true plot, terse
and open and dimensionless as $\varnothing$, the pierced cipher
falling through its own true nature, *poof,* as stars
are said to do. What stands to reason? *Entropy?*—
it goes against all sense, what's this, *the end,* per-
force, Ferris wheeling back in mind, a whorl of faces,
freed of personality, in time, maybe; but tears
stream inward, still, against the wind, centripetal.
You'll do your own recalling, friend. This periphrasis
isn't mine, it's the curve of the volume of things: moon's
swing, earth's, the stars in curving space, the petals'
whorl, the double strand, the eye of this typhoon.

*Q V S I
havc not
been able
to con Az.
wher R u*

♆

2

The End, instead, corrected first for parallax:
a log's no better than its stars, and relict
light's stale evidence. Polish the porthole's
starry zero! Listen up! Clasp its crackling earphone
closer: signal's dated still (D**r R*dr!): dirty
weather's everywhere, in the disturbed electric
field outside, or under the parietals,
where everything repeats—

*Azt
relayers
for max
locate all
ships*

                    Consider: orphaned
after doomsday, how might our computers, *T-*
minus-nought, and counting, tic tic tic, all luck
run out, repent intelligence, and curse! A poor tool
blames its workman; still, we'll have to find our
own way down this flickering decision tree,
branching, branching—

*Atz -
Clipper
190140 -
Clipper
boss says
cancell
cont plans
for trans of
pilots from
peace
makers*

Azt V amb
we will
have 1
mwb for
transfer
Dracula
not safe
for a

 The sea lies flat as x-
rays now, where the stars rise, slow and lovely. . . . Parody's
a wavy mirror, R**d*r; I ought to know; the radar
room (or rather CIC, for *Combat*
Information Center—such the lexical
effects of war!) was mine: raw light flies out, and parrots
back the world: sea surface, aircraft, paradise
kingfishers, finches, ships, all flickering—compute
the difference, MacWhirr! What's what? All echoes
signify, who knows, look now, a little cowlick
skirls across the screen, and how shall we imagine
that? We squint and study light. The universe
may be eidetic memory, but human nerve's

Suez 2 V
Malta 8
send
message
relay to
Suez
durmers
storm—pist
0 forwas

less sensitive. White flash arrives; report lags
far behind—

 Half a century, almost. Machine
intelligence ensures this peace, and I mean to observe
it. Permit me, now, to talk you back, on instrum-
ents. Relax, friend. Follow the watch: lie back: relax.

0946 Leop
V Gr. we
are now
back on
(XSC)

Imagine, once upon a time, suspended mid-
Pacific, 20,000 light-doused leagues
between the crazing lithosphere and storm-
less lilt of thinnest space, your spinning telescope
plays its backwards beacon to and fro, mad-
cap toucan taking everything in, clock-sure
eyepiece piecing together, later, out of harm's
way, some happy end:
 A young man's face, say, lifting, hopeful,
full of youth and good cheer and gratitude, admitted
suddenly to a world conditioned in this news: the luxury
of peace! *Good news! Bombs have been dropped: terms*
struck: the mechanism all disarmed.

Ψ

3

1132 Rav
V Hall
negative
present or
past

Horologium, Telescopium, Sextans. . . . Consider the storm:
of course, in the end, the rain's insane spit
and hiss lessened a little, the typhoon's coil relaxed
around us, as though the wind's own crazy piping charmed
the barometric column back. Of course, *Cobra*
was the name the Navy gave the storm—stupid
literary apotropaion, prolix
reflex, the melodramatic binding spell, armchair
jack-tars looping and unlooping rope: *abra-*
cadabra: the standing part held firmly so, the bitter
end pulls through. . . .

Quaker
Pepper was
that about
us keeping
sockeye's
planes.

                        I'll tell it that way, too, a brackish
yarn, by God—as though the thing could be *compared,*
as though the storm might in the end be bottled
like a volume: gold-tooled, lead-set, leather-
bound ephemeris for rummy old parrot-
shouldered commodores to browse, bowsprits
broken, peg-legs ticking through magnetic north—
as though the thing existed at all, apart from the purling
and tangling together of winds a little while, dispersed
long since.

Aztec Suez
Drc thinks
she should
return now
can
overtake &
make repl
Suez then
join
Volcano
stern

       I think of these things now, the whole lucky
story tangling together in memory, wreathed
in a red halo. I think of the ship's keel plunging, the spiral
shred of radar antenna turning, turning, the earth's
plates plunging under it, tumblers ticking in the little locked
vault at the end of the periodic table . . .
O hear us when we cry to thee, for those in peril
on the sea . . . and so, a spark extinguishes.
What can we know, truly? That's the trouble
with memory! And so (as yarns used to) uranium
ticks down to lead. I'll set this in hot metal,
too, and title it?—*Typhoon:* a rainy
story spun around the circumstance of terrible
knowledge watched into the world that year, the era
born, then—

♆

4
Suez 3 V
Lep We
may be the
ship to the
south of
you Screw
Q V as I
believe.
Leop to be
in that
direction

Intimations of mortality:
man's first, in fact, and coinciding with
my own. Imagine, all new constellations! *Horo-*
logium, Telescopium, Sextans, turning
in the mind's eye, rising, then—I think of these
again, and wartime, the long night watches then, a seethe
and flume of unfamiliar skies. Apparent nonsense
of it, over time, resolving. So many Southern
star-groups have peculiar names. I traced the whole filled
vault of them, at any rate, in the same shoal seas
where the first, lost, navigators of the Renaissance sought
landfall too, by the same good tools. Odd names? Why sow

Aztec V
Clipper
desire tur
cyc to
proceed
(DX-EV)
(JW-EN)
via posit
(DE-DW)
N (DWP-
WF) east
and (DE-
EWO N
(DWP-JY)
east to
search for
sun

their fresh new firmament with the gods' vaudeville
again? Begin again, with Reason! Here, at sunset
the lacquered lid lifts open to reveal, on velvet
linings, lo! bright emblems of that calibrated
intellect by which straight edge we've ruled
out earth and heaven for ourselves.

                              Geodesy,
just so: meridians raked down the ravelled
Veil, the armillary planet clappered like
an atom, ringed, unbound, her polished ferrule
snapped at last—

                    The Romance of the Deicide! *Site:*

0957 Hall
V M Screen
Raven as
he falls out
of position

Eden. Figure falls from sleep, lopes out on the hot veldt,
blinking, inks the white map motley, braiding
certain conic sections through his rolled-up fool's
cap, coasting past the moon's slow curvature, till, dizzy
with the knowledge of it all, lost, bedevilled
in the tar pit of his dreams (which, like LaBrea,
kept pitching up grotesques again, to whisper cruel
tales from the cryptic, open dossier
of mass extinction, inked in scripts such lost, devolving

0955 B2
VL3
Standby X
(XGC) CL
TA L sp
(VE) Lass4
can u pass
this mg to
lass

mirror-minded lemurs may yet scry, lip-reading
backwards off the spiral molecule, culled
genes spelled, dead sea scrolled) *till—till—*

                              O, Λ to Z
capsize the font! What yarns do the plunging dolphins
spin, wheeping and clicking their own elaborate

lingos, *ping, ping?* We can't collate
the continents, their stately, shuffling odysseys
across the spread sea floor, far less what Delphic
scrawlings limn damned chromosomes—

Aztec V Cl
your mess
in regard   Whose pied libretto
to pick up reads itself, in reprint, here: locate
Deerskin yourself, friend, if you can. Shoot the sun. Dare say
surv   *from whence,* or *whither bound . . .* it's difficult,
to say the least. The dolphin sounds.

♆

5
1042 G V
Maur 240   Such faculties
Identify as we possess, we'll try to use, then: instruments
yourself of reason, science, inspired delirium—whose tremens
is this universe, whose microwave-lit cavewall's lost, Laws
adrift, draught, where we're the Line we can't decode
and can't defend, and nearly always misconstrue—

1200 Q3
Pepp chic
from
Pepper will   As Wallace
make did a hundred years ago, by bandicoots
water and trogons, monotremes and odd koalas
landing in (lost cause, but never mind), delimiting
15 min Gondwanaland's northwesterly expansion, circa

Krakatoa. Disputed border, still: Makassar
Parlor V Strait, or Banda Sea, or split middle
Pep we of the Celebes? Lebensraum! Who cares?
check

1136 Pep V Observe again, on instruments: first, make a
I believe I circle with your compass, centered on the crosshairs
have u Wallace hatched, intersecting the equator.
(V2C) Dist Set the legs wide; twirl. The sharpened, anchored
(A) please point should leave a puncture in the map. A puff
check of steam vents out, you'll note. Epiphany
of such to come? No, label this *Tambora's crater,*

pockmarked 1815. The stone accordion
of seismic shock still hums, maybe, in the tapped earth's
mantle: it left the sky pitch dark two days; it fanned
its veil around the world—This was the year of no summer,
summer snowfall, failed crops—

                 This was the greatest explosion
in recorded history. There have been others—

Hello
Leghorn   Scan north
did u see
the crash   a few degrees, now: *Mindanao, Leyte, Samar*
swimming into view . . . identify *Luzon;*
zoom the lens in, inching east. A scattering
of ninety cockleshells should show up
presently, bobbing south in a steep chop:
this is the U.S. Third Fleet, Admiral Halsey commanding.
He does not see what you see, now: the cirrus skirt
of cloud, a little pirouette, shaping
WNW at twelve and a half knots, what will become
the most dangerous storm of the war years.

This is
Leghorn   Dial
affirm
dead   the lens in closer, here: frame the tilting oblong
ahead of of an aircraft carrier's flight deck, where crew work, coupling
Paprika planes to the catapult's slack bowstring, caught . . . too late.
Typhoon's upon them, now. The pilot's eyes dilate.

Q V Q3
Papr. is   What can we know, except what we record?
proceed to Now here's an ancient text: amidst detrital silts
crash over of fifty intervening years, I've found these pencilled
notes, the rough radio log—a wretched scrawl
in several hands, all bad—the Quartermaster's
watch aboard the *Kwajelein* kept up through the roll
and pitch of the long morning following events
I'm trying, in this poem, to recall.
Listen—

Have no
info on
leopard.   Whispers, shredding in the wind, in . . . dim Messier
Have
listened to signals, seen, miscatalogued, lost, long
his pilots since their light's winked out. Or say two hemispheres,

exchanging static, simpleminded morse
fear rattling through the first night-watching lemurs
crouching near the brain stem still, a fossil
signal, caught in a fossil seine. Song
of the land-born dolphin: who receives? Who sends?

Clipper -
Qua at pre
(Z) sockeye   You see, it's hard in places, making out the sense.
chicken on   The war was like that, though, it cast us all
board
pepepe Alto   adrift to that degree, disturbed the balance
Q make   in us, the way we keep our feet when all land's
pepper first
x return   out of sight, as though the little thimbleful
two pepper   of seawater we carry in the inner ear
pick pick
up up st   responded to the coriolis, too, the pull
pilots from   and suck all plants and hurricanes obey,
but thought—

Suez Aztec
say again   Not that: whichever hemisphere
Suez -   commands dream spun this Ancient Mariners'
Aztec neg
to last   odd melodrama next: mad Jack, the Abbot
trans stay   of Unreason's pulpit high above the nightmare
with
of the war. Whether or not the coriolis
unswirled counterclockwise, or the vessel's
screws reversed, the rule of it was turnabout,
all folly fair, all navigation visceral,
as what should lines be for, except to cross?

ψ

6
Clipper +
Atz - Mel -   Now take up instruments again: sprung watch, bent
at (QDGV)   sextant, starred kaleidoscope. Take aim. . . .
I cyc name
elephant
sighted ps   Miss.
given by   And shoot again: say roughly twenty degrees
cyc to   north latitude to twenty south, from Pearl past Fiji
scarch for
planes lat   and American Samoa, then, the shakedown cruise
(ZOQP)   acquainting me with that queer effigy
north long
(YWMEB)   of all command, connected elsewhere with Misrule,
east course   though here we called him Neptune. Those crew
(JDS) -
proc under   whose life-lines hadn't so far intersected
own power   the equator's were obliged to read his missal

82

TYPHOON

*to port but
having
trouble
over
Clipper
rodger out*

on that first occasion, taking orders
in a hazy, fool Fraternity of the Briny Deep
a good deal older than the U.S. Navy. Non-sectarian,
a salty old charade, at which the wardroom
winked, wartime permitting. Next time, Neptune turned

*1124 Bear
V
Mauradu
a target
just passed
255*

another face; but this anticipates. Adepts
gathered on the flight deck, waiting. No sextant
necessary, if we'd crossed at night, I thought, Polaris
pssst, extinguishing, its cool scintilla dipped
into the sea. . . .

*Quad v
Good Luck*

      Unsettling notion! Here green serpents' jaws,
jewelled scales coiling: coastwise sailors watched the Pillars
of Hercules awash this way, once; here we'd
left our own home waters, I was thinking—

*0908 cyc
alongside
ginger
picked up
pedro
pilots over*

                   Jostled
from the thought by greater mystery: no pelorus
but trident's needles swinging wild, in green seaweed
and not much else, *ex machina,* the god slung
up a breeches buoy and, piped aboard, bore
heaven to the deck. Ring-crusted knuckle-
bones unkissed, he closed two loony hawsepipe eyes, kelp-
caped and straightening to speak, all barnacles
and bared teeth, beard aquiver like the Gorgon's scalp,
his own adjusted with a little coral atoll,
tipped and jaunty: *now hear this!* Rum eschatology
professed by One Who Ought to Know! The quorum
of initiates assembled to a scallop
shell they'd torch-cut from an oil drum for his throne.
They blew the conch. He sneezed.

                The sailors all went prone.

♆

*7
Amt ass Q3
upon comp
of devil
report to
flag ship*

I can't recall the finer points of indecorum
any more, the ceremonial collapse
of naval discipline by rituals
which, if not altogether unfamiliar, capsized

queerly into place: here was a conning bridge
and binnacle, chronometer (two five-inch shells),
helm (a life-ring roped high), a crazy Captain
it could never answer. The true deck officers,
by custom, turned a blind eye. *Aye, Sir, no, Sir, off
with the shirt, Sir*—so the raw initiates were wrapped in
Neptune's seaweed, too, the mufti of their service
in the Underworld.

1127 Cyt V
M4 349
from me
what c are
u steering

Count 5 4 3 2 1:
the ship's keel strummed the Line. We lay still on the zero
for an instant, mayflies on a mirror's surface . . .
through. And started up the scale again, one to
twenty, ticking off the rosary
of atolls toward the Pole.

Mac-B.B.
astern
volcano sta
2

What could we know? New
Hebrides, no farther south, that trip. Espiritu
Santo might have been the Pole some half a billion
years before—the North Pole, by my charts—but no,
that island chain was molten, then; it hadn't spurted
up yet, deep from the asthenosphere. A good deal's spilled
up recently, still warm and steep, volcanoes
constellated in this circlet thirty
thousand miles around: Tierra del Fuego
west, up through the island war zones to Japan,
the arc of the Aleutians, Puget Sound, San
Diego, down the Andes, *boom*, asleep, awake,
asleep. . . . *Unparalleled on earth*, the Abbots
of Geology declaim, *a pan-
demonium of seismic violence surrounds
this blue Pacific, still, and this is called
the Ring of Fire*. There's doctrine! Think of it, this Ring
of Fire, our first ancestral Ocean, shrinking
birdbath, rocking in its rock caldera,
closing like an iris on us all,
blink—

♆

8

Bantam -
facecard
we have no   Blink: kaleidoscope: here, mark Bull Halsey's
light port   crazy eyes, deep as the bottom of the Philippine
side go   trench: staunch Admiral of the Third Fleet, whose *errors*
ahead send   *in judgement committed under stress of war operation*
your   *stemmed from a commendable desire to meet*
message by   *military commitments—*
visual

Mel V mel.   Or here, the silver, lupine
If sub   eye of a submarine commander, caught in the flat
contact is   fishbowl of its periscope, nearby. Or here, a pilot's, perched
made have   in the sun a hundred fathoms high above the fleet,
hoosegow   flight decks crawling with the tiny widow
remain   of his shadow—
with
contact till
Dory takes
over   Oh, we knew those silhouettes
                well, wingmarks like the red globes of an hour-
If Deerskin   glass, sun to sun, and nightfall sifting through the bomb-
makes   racks hung between. We saw that first in the Philippines,
contact   wide-eyed, unbelieving. How the sailors whistled
with then I   out that horror!—*skimmed in low just underneath our*
instruct   *radar's skirt, curved up* (a steep climb, open palm)
him to   *just hung there for a second, rolled, and—*
ridur torr

                                          Silt
0622   on the seafloor, now. Now joined by other vessels
Emerg 110   lost that night, in the whorl of the radar's green eye. . . .
turn

Quad V do   Old
you know
where B   notes. Old seas grown calm in a slick of fusel
                oil. From here, I calculate the steady sift
                of diatoms and fine volcanic ash
                will smooth this over in a million years, drift
                that dead squadron's hangar deck with newer fossils,
                before it slips down underneath the Asian
                mainland—
0627
above   Men's bones in the mantle of the earth! Fault
repeated   lines, followed down, followed back, from the Great Rift
we are   Valley to this present pass, at the far sill
returning   of the tipped Pacific plate, the world's first ocean
to area to   basin, staring down the black storm's rifled
make   barrel, crazy for our enemy, scarcely
another
search

85

feeling the barometer, the low whistle
in the whelk shell spiraling around us then—

Mel Clippr
V Aztec if
evolution
of
Scalawag
is sub
cyclones
cover til
Dory take
over

                                           I've filled
the blanks since then, or tried, to plot what course
carried us that Advent season through the cross-
hairs of catastrophe.

$$\psi$$

9
0620 Mel
V
Scallywag
making
sound
contact
now

            Coordinate again: Xmas
Eve six days away, Luzon to starboard
some three hundred miles, the Marianas
off to port, Poles both fore and aft, and moon
above and sea below—and soon, amidst
eleven dozen rhumb lines winding on the arbor

Mel V
Slwag lost
orig
contact am
scarching
area

of a *severe tropical disturbance* closing on us
quickly, then—

              Unruly winds. Not yet *typhoon.*

Bear V
Quaker5
take posit
in Quaker
formation

I didn't so much wonder then (as Nimitz
must have) how it happened, how the *most*
powerful fleet in the world was allowed to blunder to its
greatest loss without compensatory return
since the first Battle of Savo (vide CinCPac,
13 February, 1945). . . . That ink's
still running, by my watch: and still the thought occurs
one might as well decoct another shook tureen
too full of croutons, solve Savo's last position
drifting through its primal broth of jostling islets,

1140 B3 V
S3 X to foll
2 turn
MBack

lost or salvaged ovcr time, replot the course
Quiros took: what *incognita,* white terrain!

Screwball I
am unable
to make
that turn I
can not get
over there
at pres

Sealed orders. Torres slit them open. Thus commissioned,
parted from his flagship by a squall (as we were), Pilot
Torres took command, weighed anchor at Espiritu
Santo, set his helm southwestward, bearing
for Gondwanaland—

                         Which, bearing north itself,

TYPHOON

Arc (PRC)
Dist (XE):
if we are
unable to
stay
together
today we
will w

its own outriding island arcs already piled
up, smoking, on the Sunda Shelf—appears to
splinter into Asia while we watch, the fair-
ways closing, just as Torres slips between. Here twelve-
wired birds of paradise and paradise kingfishers,
fairy loris, forest kangaroos, the ANZAC
corps of bandicoots and flightless cassowaries
hold the Line Lord Wallace drew (with barbet quills
and cockatoos) across such gerrymandered fissures,
shear-lines, sunk subduction zones, as zig and zag
this poor blue eggshell of a world. . . .

Quaker5 -
Quaker
Roger
rejoin

                                   So, wary
of a hostile landfall, jungle drums, the squall
sky a stretched komodo dragon's hide

Scally wag
leaves fm
center of
formation

patched orange here, now here, with the glare of signal
fires that trace his passage, Pilot Torres steers hard
by the shore in a narrow strait. Crooked arrows
arc and clatter on his decks—

0950-BI V
S Keep
clear of
Elepant pls
7 ack

                              Advance the spark:
the Philippines ahead, MacArthur's own head-
hunters landing, fragrant aerosols
of flame are billowing like ectoplasm
from the troopers' hands, hissing through the dark
cave-mouths where snipers hide and breathe until their oxygen
is gone—

Canary - Q
Roger do
you have
Hell-D or
avenger Q
- C Wait.

                       Retard the spark, and lo! it rustles
in a nest of tinder here, in the chasm
lit since Africa: here Java Man squats, gently
teasing fire from stone, to trace his sojourn
here, now *here*, now *here*, the candelabrum
of our history—

Gr V Leop
There are
ships
astern of u
V We now
have fire
under
control

                      Now blow it out. Blackout.
The Spanish captains' claims, the aborigines',
MacArthur's line, Lord Wallace's, Tambora's broomed
chimney smoking, snowfall in Vermont, a cloud-
glow sheeting over Eniwetok, tic toc, *boom.*

ψ

10

Q V Blue
Dev Test
empty life
preserver
close
aboard no
personel
abord

Begin in June of '44: this is the *Kwajalein's*
commissioning. We stand respectfully. The joystick's
pulled back hard in the chaplain's rhetoric; he's *called*
the Lord to bless us just as thou didst bless
the Ark of Noah riding out the flood . . . which, island-
bound as we were in our own logistical
support work with the Third Fleet (ballasted
with fighter planes instead of, as it were,
the world's genetic patrimony) catapulted
its fair share of miseries, alas,
back up the buzzing loggias of the sky. . . .

Brownee V
Max how
many
planes
have u to
transfer

                                              I'd preach
the whole high sermon out, here, fill the wide blue choir-
loft full of smoke, and fail, still. Say less: say we pelted
heaven with replacement parts, each piloted
by some young man we'd swung aboard by breeches
buoy a day or two before, plucked back the highwire
on a fresh airframe around him, waved, and pulled
the lanyard—*whoosh!* another fighter hooked offstage
and skittering across our radar screens to stitch
and purl what bluest yonders constitute a War
Department's dreams.

Clipper
Brass say
N to that
prop do
not trans
pilots from
the small

                                  Ah, those, of course, we weren't
allowed to share. We were a cause—to what effect?
A life of details, by and large, logged. *Item: starch*
goes rancid in the tropics, laundry sweet as mummy-
wrappings clinging in the heat. The elevator
deck is fine for volleyball. Neptunis Rex:
we cross the Line. Item: the enemy
has started using suicide—so, late or
soon, we all have done, God save us now, no olive
branch borne in on a sweet land wind—*Item: Timor,*
Leyte, Yap, Luzon, Saipan, Noumea,
Pearl again, Guam. The fleet steams north. *Item:*
typhoon.

Ψ

11

by, gr V
Leop. sig
course give
you better
riding or
not over

Imagine if you will a hundred twenty war-
ships held in close formation, like confetti
in a closed fist, tossed (to strain this metaphor)
by a blood-and-glory gold-braid admiral
imagining maybe he'll get himself brevetted

0940 Gyp,
gr V Leop
How will
new course
change
make u
ride

down in History by square-jawed, squint morale
alone, as though the sheer exercise of will
could countermand the senses' evidence, the loosened
winds unsacked here, howling, new rain riveting
the sky's streaked plate down hard against the sea's. . . .

Leop V gr.
I believe I
will ride
better on
pres course
than
course

When visibility was zero, still, the whorled
pupil held its own horizon: *strike Luzon:*
resume offensive operations: strike Luzon.
The words repeat three times in Halsey's
testimony later, for the inquiry.

0845 Leop
VS no,
keep in
touch and
if visibility
clears
rejoin us.

Under obligation to strike . . . that thought . . . uppermost
in our heads right up to the last minute—

When the world immersed.

0843 S
V04 eng
trouble,
main
motors
grounded.
trying to
isolate
trouble.
We are not
able to go
ahead at
this time

It was too late! But what's the truth here? True, Fleet Weather
Central misconstrued this storm. The Horn Book Quiros
likely carried quotes the necessary clues,
vidi Knight, or Bowditch—better augurs, either,
one, than the broadcasts Halsey listened to. *What Laws*
cyclonic gods abide by must needs be obeyed,
our Chaplain might intone here, quite correctly: *A:*
then, stitch the air with horizontal rain; *B:* braid
a cross-swell on the water, syncopating
pitch and roll; *C:* drop the ship's barometer

0946 Leop
V gr we
have temp
lost
steerage
control will
regain as
soon as
poss

three hundredths of an inch an hour. Very well,
a typhoon's on the way.

And O, the open vowel
of that storm's round center formed and veered
directly through the fleet—as though such grommets
in a word alone could pluck this line and purse

0946 Leop
V Gr. we
are now
back on
(XSC)

this page I'm inking into singularity, the way the whole
sky warped and crumpled in that night, immense
and shredding tarpaulin torn round and turbanned
in close, and last light gone, all clarity

89

1003 S V
Raven we
have
steering
casualty

gone—and still Halsey held to the term *disturbance.*
That's the word the Admiral persisted
with, all through that first, sudden, terrific night, the burst
hydrant of the second day—

ψ

12
1005 Leop
V Gr I am
unable to
main
course. I
am
starting to
loose my
deck
clothes

At 13:45,

at last, the Admiral radioed the word *typhoon.* The *Spence*
had sheared in half two hours before; the *Monaghan*
and *Hull* had sunk: three ships, with 98 survivors;
seven hundred ninety men were dead—

The mind spins—

1009 S4
Leop V
Leop Did u
get my last
xmiss That
c will run
u into
Grizzly

My own station was the radar room. Recall the sweep hand
scything on the screen all night, recall the man on
duty watching the blip's green blear
and wipe and blear and wipe, where suddenly before
his eyes one lightpoint winked and disappeared. . . .

1018
Icebox-St v
Leop I am
to the right
C (AJO)
1021 Q V
Vet we just
passed CVL
c(EPO)

And then we raised our prayer to Neptune/Mananaan
MacLir/Almighty God—how might the customary
sermon run? say: *Lo! It happened then the sun*
broke, the mad seas calmed, our comrades were restored
to us . . .

They weren't, of course. Whatever immanence

R V ship
115 we
have no
steering
control
stand clear

of light-in-ocean tossed Odysseus once (like Timor,
Kai, New Guinea, Eniwetok, Guam, Luzon)
up high and drying in the air, ignored the roster
of that capsized ship, that night.

B4 V Elep I
had to I
am now
heading

Kyrie Eleison!

Capsize! The mind's own righting moment, timor mortis,
keeps these thoughts abstract, mathematically austere
as thirty-nine degrees of roll, or twenty tons sustained

Q - C.
Negative

wind pressure bearing on the smokestack; eighty, laced
in gusts near the storm's hollow eyelet: here all leafstraw

tears away: wings come off the planes; planes, collapsed
and tumbling loose on deck, get jettisoned; fire spurts,
spreads, whoosh, slakes in a great wave. So, lopsided,
plunging, propellers cavitating air, we lost our
steering, hove to in a trough, tossed, and didn't capsize,
and didn't break in two.

ψ

13

*1032 I
have lost
all control
heading
250*

                        All night I watched the eddying
of radar waves across the screen, thoughts through a cyclops'
light-lanced mind, *identify! Identify!*—

*1036 Gy V
Leop I am
hove to
also*

                          Say Gloucester,
or the cracked Fool. Say Noah, when the icecaps
melt again, green water thundering

*1038 S V
Eleph I
believe
CVE SB
NE of this
ship*

each ventilation shaft and stack and clapped
hatch and human throat and every other closed
tube of blue sky left unfilled in the flood and the seismic
whorl of things—

*1041 Q V
Vet we
turned to
avoid CVE
we arc ret
to c now.*

                   Mad Song's a hoary, old, enduring
trope; this *Victory at Sea* tone, too. No aptitude
for melodrama, though, no flair for pyroclastic
language ever matches such events. Mix
Melville, Conrad, Shakespeare—storm-mongers, Abbots
of Unreason, each one, factoring what terms

*1046 We
believe the
CVE in our
midst is
Gypsy*

his theorem of Misrule might plausibly abide
by: God's rage? Entropy? The unsolved stomach's
dread knot, tightening. What's information? π
r^2, or *Lear*, or *isobars* and *isotherms*
logged in on the same torn chart? What can we know about
these things? *True:* heart ratchets on the same watchstem
Andromeda does. *False.* What are the terms?
What can we know of the nature of circular storms?

ψ

14

1048 This
is Gypsy
dead in
water have
my
searchlight
going over

I've since seen radar images, the storm's green churn
and pinwheel, photographed, fixed. As though that orbit
might be plotted after all, as though, in turn,
it might be turned in memory, and brought to focus
like a lens.

0915 face
card v
aztec—give
brief report
your
cond—rep-
ort both
steering
motors out
(steer by
hand)
emerg
diesel out
FB anten
wreacted
numbers
radio
anten 2
down 36"
searc light
stippes long
frame split
in two
inches after
deck hous
buckled
both side 6
holes main
deck
forward
wheac
stanch
carried
away

No visibility. The gusts
drove spray so hard the bulkhead paint pitted
and stripped. The flight deck was swept repeatedly;
green water over the navigation bridge. Lookouts
pulled from their stations in the forward catwalks. Gouts,
plumes with each steep plunge; the ship's screws lifted
high. Below, worse: eyebolts sheared, and planes adrift
in the squat sky of the hangar deck, hot wreckage screeching
back and forth with each roll, back, forth, catching fire,
fog nozzles writhing in the sailors' hands, and each hatch
bleeding fresh seawater down to mix in the shin-
deep sluice of brine and oil and trash and aviation
fuel, electric cable cut and popping here and there—

And through it all, like drunken, Sisyphean herons thrash-
ing and spraddling some gimballed, blue-spark-lit, prim-
ordial marsh our racial memories won't drain, each mortal
sailor threw his weight against the ship's: now uphill
on the port roll, now uphill back—a whole crew, pell-
mell, by their Captain's orders! Queer, nightmarish
memory. Bosch, say: red-rover, in Hell. A quickmarch
history by Tolstoy, say: *alas,*
men of the East! men of the West! shifting ballast
on a flat, tilting plate, say?—twirling on a broomstick,
balanced on a juggler's furrowed brow. . . .

started
king post
boom
damad
beyond
repair 100
ft main
deck life
rails
carried
away &
one boat
badly
dam-
aged—over
M8 wilco

Doom's-
day, that's the book, our story's epicenter
from the very start. Man's fate, surveyed,
as usual, without good instruments: *tic,*
toc, the screen sweeps blank again: land's end:
dread reckoning, by fireflies flecked and braided
on a fitful night breeze, where the mind reenters
sleep, and tries again to orient
itself, and fails. Purblind, a new flash not yet fading

0920
goodluck
Quak can
discharge
of motor
gear task
be delayed
until dark
from our sheeted retinas, where the optic nerve wicks
starfire to the brain, we blink the ember
back again, and come awake again, afraid.

♆

15
1118
Beaver V
Archer
man
overboard
from
Archer on
port side
What can we know? What bearings can the newly wakened
eye decode? Caught light: here's murmurous REM
sleep, flickering again its addled sums: *works,*
days: somewhere near or over the current pole, an AWACS
dome is humming through the clouds, remembering.
Below the icecap, cat or mouse, a submarine, *ping,*
holds its breath, banks the fires in its reactors,
drifting sideways, listening. Between, the wreathed
Pole itself has wobbled south a hand's breadth
since I started writing this.

1110
Raven V
calling
ship (Y) M
we have no
steering
control
                                        Log *item:* bearing
off as if to intercept the United States Third
Fleet (fighting for its life in the dropped mercuric core
of a *severe tropical disturbance,* 18 December,
1944) the Imperial Nipponese
Home Islands steam south through the China Sea. MacArthur's
saucer-eyed ancestors, holding beachheads, sabertooths
and mastodons and sun bears and Sambar
deer beside them, sleep. A forest canopy
creeps over their horizon to the south, thyrsii
in the distance, palm-tops tossing in the hazy Tethys
Sea, where only water was before . . .
a New World. Tea in a stoneware pannikin,
set in a bed of coals.

Q3 V Pep
we just
passed life
raft with 3
persons in
it
                                So here's the Ring of Fire
again, our red-rimmed ocean's history: here's Torres,
storm-tossed, separated from his captain, sailing
on sealed orders across white parchment, bound
for haven at Luzon. His heart's desire,
the great Southern Continent, restores
itself in terraces around him: here the Sahul
Shelf rides in and splinters hard aground,
ahoy!—*here,* and *here,* and *here,* and *here,* Spice

93

Islands, land in all directions!—held whole
again in a brass test tube, a lost navigator's spy-
glass, say, or orbiting computer's compound,
glittering, kaleidoscopic eye, where the earth's crazed
tesserae, piled up here since the Pliocene,
play light back through the mind. . . .

Melody V
Raven: Just so, the pied
have got periodic tables; just so, mosaic
message
complete photographs; just so, the nicked genes, spliced
from Suez and healed, and twirled, annealed, to thread this maze
3 tlwirk V misruled as memory in time—
out

ψ

16
1119 Fairc
V B4 Take   *Item:*
action here is new mathematics. *Item:* Tambora
man
overboard blows a hundred cubic miles of firmament
from back up into the sky. The rising plume twirls
Archer twice around the earth. New England farmers
watch snow fall on cut hay in July. Hard frost
each month, all year, that year; they drop their tools
and take the railway west. The land goes back to aspen,
pine. . . .

0847 Q V   And here the flightless rails walk westward too,
no sign of dry-footed to New Guinea. Here in an upland forest
life on that
raft in a green, West Gondwana summer, cycads and horsetails
wave in a mild land breeze, and a Spanish captain spins
slowly on his anchor chain, and the first
flowering plants on earth unfold in the saucer
of the daystruck lemur's eye. . . .

V Archcr   And here the circinations
wc have
recovered of a tropical disturbance turn all thoughts
our man together, as dream does, waterspout
and telescope collapsing at a single point,
and none of this the least bit to the point: *that*
year new knowledge came into the world. . . .

1128 Atz V   Zero,

we have   period. End of message. First, though, Reader, part
mess on
channel c   these waters once more, before the ink-penned
memory snaps shut for good, and zoom
your lens in close. Earth, here, blue spark on sere
space. Here the round Pacific, original loom
where lively molecules spun out one afternoon, some
years ago. Here a fleet, circling in a skein
of wrong coordinates, old charts, misruled.
Here one plucked line singing, where the steam catapult
fires again, forever, a young pilot's face caught

—req.   in the grimace of acceleration, lips pulled back, skin
unchanged draped hard on the bones of the skull, dials spooling,
end of   time pluming off the watchface, blue sky palled
messeag
Clip V. Gr with storm and time, in the mind's eye, shrinking to
ack.   receive him.

♆

*

Bottlefly on God's
cheek, orbiter, O
arbiter, pronounce
now what nascent con-
stellation's marsh-
light leeches here—
not in the ruck
and heave of sky, but
here on the veer
curve of the round cloud-
forest of heaven!

*

O, Father, this
discovery revokes
the past. Project
a future for it,
torse and fret:
recheck the white
chart's web, dead-
reckon this non-
sequitur turned *thus*
or *thus* in memory:

*

*

Or where are traces
of the future? Chart
it, orbiter: to borrow
time, wind this stem: turn
earth, thyrse axis slant
through cirque ecliptic *toc*
tic—O rare Reader!
ratchet forward, past this
play apocalypse, cupped *just*
so, its pocked dust
and cracked toy orrery
reshuffling unlit stars—

*

Which? *Siva the Destroyer*, then,
that cobra blink?
Or *Lucifer's* cold fusion's flame?
The Riddle's seive?
The Scythe's swathe?
Thy myth omits hypotheses, Lord:
echolocate: ink thy name

*

*

O, *wilco,* cog-
wheel scarecrow!—look,
where thy dipped quill
detects incoming text:
already ink and color,
gold-leaf, vine-bloom:
whole skulleries
of radars stacked
below the icecap,
catchments set
for the missiles lacy uncials
scrolling overhead,
illuminating

*

Nothing:
O, maker, ink in no
thing, this is crowned
unreason, sin, the iris
of the red garotte: not
Autumn, if fall: omega's
caul curve pursing, so: the smoke-
ring's subscript here sky-
written on the crypt,
christening us all,
and counting

*

☽
♂
☿
♃
♀
♄
☉

*

Bat-ear, orbiter,
tic: turn, then
chip and bit,
titanium antennae
slipped deep this
side of death,
threaded catheter
through the sky's waste past,
pierce
this moot future, too: touch
the open membrane's
braille: the live
leaping nerve of
never never never

*

Navigate
thyself, Father:
thread the wick
back through the flame:
these intermittent light-
bursts, random,
dim, die,
and only constellate
in tiered time,
in memory,
and even here
they have no name.

*

Lucifer

Round and round, then, and ever contracting towards the buttonlike black bubble at the axis of that slowly wheeling circle, like another Ixion I did revolve

1
Up,
Down

Z: sleep's letter, little lightning zig to earth:
orthography stops here, Reader; so the plane
geometers did once; so too will you. Explain
it all in *n* dimensions if you can. The theory's
solid, anyway, in three. A keystroke
on the universal simulator demon-
strates—
   Tic:
      Blank computer screen lights up. Plan *X*
appears (recrossing Lethe, so to speak), orthog-
onal, now tipping to a crucifix. A cuestick
spindles through the origin, just *there:* a dim,
six-pointed, jack-shaped star! By which light Adam
once upon a time punched in his own damned author's
note, as Lew would, later—
        Ssst into the Styx—
and live to tell this tale, which I, in other
words, tell you: *up, down,* plumb: please denote
the axis of this story—
      Space bar, asterisk—
all stories, maybe, coming down to it: the weird
of the frogman caught in free fall, heart on ether. . . .

There's suspense for you! All four coordinates
reduced to one, this poor, point creature caught athwart
time's flow, thrown half across the bar—
        And River
City never mind, sin doesn't enter it
these days, quite otherwise; it's just the earthward
way of things.

       ☜

2
God's
Ape

     Think: whiskey *(xx),* sex *(x,y),* pool,
dice—all vice is up or down like these. Our veering
orrery's rewound, a world's short fall to winter
modelled here in a deck of chips and circuit cards.
Observe the newly hatched machine, mulish, spooling
half-wit, winking—what?—mathematical vivarium
where whole ecologies collapse or don't, and wonder-

105

working icons weep or don't which augured
Götterdämmerung's graphed in—
                              This fireman's pole
to hell, this greased abscissa through the sine wave, verm-
iform as we'll soon be—
                              X marks *that* spot, interred
in time, hid ahead in the starry dark. . . .
Turn off the screen. This dirt's reversible;
there's software for you! Corse and plot, eternity's
at hand, friend, and who has terms for that? *Etc.,*
you'll say? A grease spot on the radar dish, *dah-*
dit, tin phone to the monkey's ear! O sibyl-
lance of far light, firelight's fiber optics, souter-
rain to empyrean, Reader!—*blink, blink,* a pulsar's
hopeless Paul Revering, dictees taken from the dark garden,
gravity, adumbrated once more by black arts
into another cursed cosmogonic satyr
play—
            And this one, too, begun with apples
falling, the click of billiard balls gone wrong . . .
                                             God

ends up verisimilar, steep down the decimal
somewhere, dicing quarks in a heavy water's
wet, hot heaven. That's the text, taken simple.
Make it sing!

⚛

3
To   call it.
Gravity   Pome falls, on cue. Curtains,
         Later, if the Green Room still exists, we'll spill
some cheer across the deep, observe the old Headwaiter's
hand, the silver trays held steady, high, hell's hollow
stems up, pinched and ringing—
                              Down the hatch! A tinker's
dam for the last math solving apes for angels: gospel
goes false, always, sulphur in the nose, or neutron
star collapsing through its own naught's noose into the holy
O and mystery again—
                    Poof, no more trinity
of forces for you. Bottoms up! The tell-
tale always whiffs this way, that's gravity—

Salute,
then: *to gravity!* That latex safety net,
elastic grid graphed in across this little holo-
caust of watts and volts that veil machine intel-
ligence—
      L—
         (Enter angel's name:)
                  A silhouette
spins past again, slow motion, on the monitor.

⚜

4
Masque
    Don't think about it, Reader. Run up the martini
flag, another ensign flown, unreason's—
                     Say how Lew
looked, *X* against the firmament, and no more net, or
ever?—raise a glass and try to focus: still no
telling? Take this story then, simulated in loose first
person at a floating point six feet or so from the torse
at the center of its field: a swizzled nautilus
of silk or gas against God's chest, a blue blaze, Lucifer
struck *scratch* against the dark, as *ssst*, celestial
mechanics pirouettes 2D through a bright computer's
terse silicic mind today, to catch the natal
instant fresh: *thus*, it was *thus*—and oh, the sapphire
of that first morning!

             So the stale laws
leave us: figurative, pure, illustratory
truth: the first seed dropped, the last dark satellite
dropped rolling round the shallow dish of its receiver,
software watching—what? say ancient solstice
fires which leapt and flashed and signalled news of lost Troy
home, *boom*, and half the letters of the Iliad
expropriated for the math.

            Thus, volatile
as always, old Zeus Thunderer, *Who durst dis-*
turb the universe (voice over, so: our atl-
atl intellect tossed free of flesh at last):
                 Trees
branched then by the logic of their roots, and who—foresee

yourself!—came brachiating through the understory?
Here's no writer nor no reader either, raddled
in the ROM chip *tic:* a masked narrator, face-
plate fogging, *O,* the vatic versifier's
rising breath? Or else? Or still less subtle
chorus *toc* caught, with you, too, Reader, ill at
ease inside this odd, toroidal cipher
of a broken conversation. . . .

❧

5
The
Plan

                Surely inner
space can give us this much back! Celestial
mechanics must be this: one true roulette
the eyeball bounces by, the way the shell's
fit back on addled heaven once for all: inertial
Law—
        Or if not truth, what, then? A tool? List
others, then: tall tales, which rule the night, and let
us nod, and sleep. . . .

                Just so: a blue sky settled
on our shoulders, once, I'll say. And then the planet
fell to us again, a landfall, so to
speak, a windfall. Well, all satellites
describe this arc, according to the plan—

Where earth, too, dimples space, a blue-green artificial
olive in its tumbler, star-spritz, soda—
dizzying!—just like the fall, firsthand.
                Or *plunge,*
rather; we were frogmen after all, on a high shoal.
This was our first training jump. *Ordovician,*
I was thinking, devolving there in the silver plane's salt
bucket: cold as prime numbers we sat
packed in close in the glow of the dull jump-
light—
        Lucky as a sun, that looked, a lively suit,
like hearts—
             Ace of flame! Acetylene
and oxygen together in the breast, too lean
a mixture, first, for light, held at the howling doorjamb

of the vacuum . . .
                            Eons later, blood ran richer,
let's say, recapitulating by the dozen such offset
ascents as mind seems capable of sketching
here, between the azure Cambrian and windy Kitty-
hawk. Dogma; still, gills or wings, all creatures
drop. There's never been a net, but wind. We'd
have to spin our own from seed, *up, down,* weighed
down—

6
The
Oldest
Dream

                    And this anticipates: *tic, toc,* it
all comes back to me, in spades: the dark reach
up, Venus appearing to rise as we rose, false
dawn breaking at a thousand feet to dawn . . . the target
zone. A flight of finny heroes down! So each
man throws the bones, his own shadow cast down hard
against the turning earth, I think. So night falls
fast, like sediment, and so, a sheaf of shades
all fluttering the single common dream, come true,
did we—
                    Is this the oldest dream? oh, the heart
floods in the babe's chest in the dam's womb, and always
will, to this, till moon and stars have ricochetted
across the last human eye the last time—

                                        Time extrudes
two ways in mind, and this comes back: the waltz
of divers down that darkened corridor, all packed
in chest-to-back in full regalia, wet suits, tanks
and all, the engine noise, the bay doors shuddering
into the wind—
                    Like so much seafood aspic
quaking in an aluminum mold, we held our
protoplastic shape against the odds, the angst
of the fledged amphibian, gamely shouldering the air.

  I checked my pressure gauge again, its arrow
fixed at full, a stopped clock face. I checked my halter
straps, and hoisted up the stubby, cold, bald
wings, and thought *how many cubic yards of sky*

109

to harness on a single man! imagining my narrow
shoulders feathering a flock of seagulls, bottled
there, and following the pressure front down. I
told the countdown, then, the *10* to *9* to *8*
7, 6, 5, 4, tic toc to *0,* then *Roger—*
Go—

  Geronimo—

⸎

7
           If this anticipates,
The well, numbers always do! Who'd deny
Num- a normal interest in the nature of that naught
bers through which one half perceives one's personal erasure,
pulse at the ringed wrist like a watch-capped castanet,
or rhythm through the meter, or round muscles at the iris
or the cervix leaking roe or silk or God
knows what-all auguries, or us: as Zoroast-
rian magicians watched while one Polaris
scribed its little geared gyre across race
memory, the pupil's dark garotte
snaps shut too above a false horizon's razor-
grass in the breezy missile fields of Dakota
(coalsacks like Lascaux, where Raven on a pole spills
night across another simulation) so: Polaris
hanging in the dead eye of some computer nested
in its needle underground, ahead, to guide
it over the ice-pack, home.

       And oh, there's a chill,
limited intelligence!—any loris,
any tarsier who turns his eyes, his great, nascent
saucers-full of heaven inward, seems less innocent
than that. But then, who knows how in its differential
curve and mystery this world approximates
itself in mind? Apprenticed to some sorcery
of ones and zeroes, zeroes, ones, what fresh if
shallow vision may man's single sentient child
achieve? The whole fantasia? Stop:

        Rock simmers
under a new sun. Earth, a bun in the computer,
cools. Continents take shape, and drift. The shelved thesaurus

of dead reptiles rages past, troll-yawn
and belch below a lost land bridge. . . .

                              A pewter
pool of water, fringed with reeds, wrinkled
with the least rainbow suggestion of petroleum
beneath. A bubble, rising, sends out rings
which gently lap the shore. The air hums prettily,
like bees, as cybernetic buzzards raise an
eery gobbling cry for the magnetic spirit
of some thirsty ungulate that came to drink
and, fastened in its own reflection, disappeared
behind the veil of this queer, black event horizon,
singularity, the tar pit—

                  Period.
And so another mass extinction, spilled ink,
etc., what runs across this page, and dries.
All history is punctuated so, the green flash, parrot-
flicker fading on the monitor, in paradise,
if this is green, if this is anything
at all, that breaks inside us too, in rings,
or breaks above us in our dream like one bad prayer,
parsing time to zero in our eyes.

                           ☞

8   Reduce
Sight   this sun-sight to its point: dimensionless, the dark decimal
Reduc- mole on the leaping Morris dancer's cheek: small
tion   thing, ring remnant of the whole starry canopy—

                                        Or
so the story goes: *once, long ago, this dancer's*
face was altogether black . . . one pir-
ouette recalls another, Reader: simulacra
ring this firelight, too, red eyes the damned deuce
our poor machine can't reason through, peering through what
leaves or stars remain, to save appearances:
another loony masque enacted under silicon
like Darwin's uncle's finchless old Botanic
Garden, diaphanous gods stumping among its ferns and lichen-

crusted metaphors—why, here's Old Nick,
I think! An antlered man; a bird-masked man; an abbot
and an ape. You couldn't conjure sillier
equations with a constant cosmological as Scratch
himself. Still, how distinctly simian the leer
our constellated sky gives back! And still
we study it in costume, when we're serious.

Here's greasepaint. Blacken your own cheeks. Ratchet
forward past the dawn of time and dinosaurs
and so forth, back into that airborne instant over
water—listen, aluminum rivets *rat-a
tat* in wind outside, us huddled in the propwash
off the sweep hand of the navigator's stopwatch,
waiting for the red light's timely, dilatory shift: half
of half of half. . . .

         And I, like some poor ratite
twice extinct already, accidentally heaven-
sent, some thunderous mudfoot moa, some defunct elephant
bird aloft again and losing airspeed, stuck
in free fall, hung fowl on the short hook of the hyphen
in between, *tic-*

9
Jump!   *Toc:* I listened then, the static
lines (our ripcords clipped on a running wire) clicked
one by one like worry beads, or water
flowers threaded on a string—and then I saw
the man in front of the man in front of me turn
green, and gone, a sleek reluctant otter
on the mudslide, *chop,* a black blood sausage
link sliced loose and falling, heart, altimeter
unwinding in the sun toward what lost ancient
chain of rotifers and diatoms turned atolls
untold centuries and just four hundred yards
below, oh Acheron! and if the carburetion
of these metaphors seems rich, how odd
is that, I ask? It's like the world, why, in the addled
instant, Humpty-Dumpty's mind involves a milliard

blown bulbs, that swollen moment just before
the future goes to shards. All linkage
to the future's fragile; all such failures fear
anticipates—
                    And still the blue, lapsarian
condition catches us off guard!—*Ellipsis*
points, interrobang—

                              OK: the aqualung
I carried on my back was light as air
then, and an ill wind in my throat, I felt
the wind then, and a green light flashed and filled
the window of my mask, and I stepped through—

10 Parachute Fails

                                                  No language
adequate to what comes next. No nightmare
ever spun so slowly on its spindle
as those shrouds around Lew's feet. Was darkness folded
at the shoulder blades too carelessly? Which
word-problem is physics of this sort? A simple
prose declarative, *eg: assume a point*
mass L, in a perfect vacuum. A: a gallows
trap springs open. B: rope sings. C:—
                                             What happened? Tell
it straight for once: *up, down:* the principles
of falling aren't so fucking difficult:
the last weight out the window's last to earth—
                                                      By Gali-
leo's notes, not these! You solve it: what's intel-
ligence but formal syntax, anyway? A symbol's
crash, a Turing tape's hiss, a faculty
no ghostlier than hopscotch of the spheres, the legal-
istic tropes of Mars, the whole galactic
hand-crank organ-grinder's dissassembly:
blip: an intuition traces sand like Foucault's
plumb bob curving down the umpteen local
non-Euclidian anomalies emburled
in mind or sky since Einstein left it all unstarched.
Here's Nature's egg, cryptography, that pure fool's gold,

good code, that's all. When lo! that logic gate's small guil-
lotine snaps shut at last, what, like an embolism
drifting through the skull of the sleeping chimpanzee
might blink awake with *Lucifer,* the morning star,
rising here along a microchip's Z
intercept—

> A conscious zero!—

> > Towards which, inching
by discrete states, William Tell's ballistics
exercise proceeds, as—

&

**11
Re-
serve
Para-
chute
Coll-
apses**

> O, *Principia!*
Machine intelligence, my ass! A model
of the mind, indeed, redshifting every apple
listed in the great Programmer's dream, each operand
a guppy bubble bumped *tic* down its little metal
bench in the blue nitrogen of an excluded middle,
my word, Reader, heaven knows there's a good deal more to
all of this than gargling up a bleat of witless
ones and nothings in a digital array. The records
specify *malfunction.* Whose? The silkworm's mortal
sin, evolving, or the first Jump Master's? Lew's? What
can one calculate except that this *occurred,*
contingent on a plan hatched out of anti-
space eight months before to join the Navy Seals?
Who knows how qualities of mind or nerve or soul
subvene? Imagine an old-fashioned hero: who'd in
a hundred years have picked this man for the joker
in a dropped deck? Still, I'll recognize the silhouette
again, as he goes by, trussed up like poor Houdini
in a lead belt, so, and a great, white, luffing windsock
losing altitude as if it were the checkered
flag for—

> Say again: what semaphore's forgotten
here, what flapping arms or flags or winking sequinned
messages send this thought home?—

> > Oh, I can't hope
to tell it straight, but dream it still, along the ripcord's
first, failed geodesic, then the second, whiffling drogue—

the safety chute's white stream and sudden canopy—
then *whooosh!* the whole silk collapsed back down, flew
down between Lew's legs like God dropped a brick
in it.

&

12
The
Third
Law

Begin descent. You'll need another drink,
Dear Reader—
            Barkeep—
                        This part's scary and opaque in
points of fact and physically demanding. Lew's
role reifies ellipticality, baroque,
a recreative wire-whisk in the perfect eyecup
of the Renaissance—you'll get the picture. Kepler
drew it first in the sands of Mars, in the nave
of Newton's dream, not four centuries before the rocket's
white roke rose on the same curve there . . .
                        The Epic
of our Age, Part II, correct? Kept blurred
in simulation, here, where the blown dioptric nerve
of the falling monkey's crossed its contrail: track
it! Fill that flat reflector's glass! Here's drunken, Luddite
trig for you, your chance to re-derive the Third
Law gone all dithyrambic and abandoned, *Pan trog-*
lodytes indeed, dunce cast down the old chthonic
sections, *x,y* on the thyrsus—

                        Think:
the earth leapt up to Lew as Lew fell!

                        Fact. So mothered
in the dawn of that conjunction, the awful
get of Newton's Law on Darwin's myth—
the brute creation *thus,* and clayfoot rook-
eyed fabricator falling skyward off
all fours—that's the story, isn't it?—white-eyed, terror-
struck, scruff-slung down this long, interrogatory
drop into *intelligence,* or *conscience?*—
consciousness, or *science,* was it?—still we'll conjure
heaven as we have to, talk and hat trick, half tre-
panned.

115

⚘

13
The
First
Flower-
ing
Plant

　　　　　As this masque, too, may likely be—its rocket-
opera premises and technomantic jargon,
chintz and velvet, vulgar charm and butler's pantry
sound effects—as though the great dome's inner
shell were thus! awash with our reflection, groggy,
cupped between two furry palms, gonged (cheers!)
once again against Zen-Puritan preponder-
ating taste:

　　　　　Unreason, Reader! All inertial
guidance fails! All ceilings are baroque
at 40,000 feet, by God!—the turbine
whirring full of geese, the crazy terrapins
and pilot whales scrabbling up the shingle's shaly
pitch—
　　　　　Where wave-and-particle are pure Tarot:
the Morris man's white, energetic gyre, the Abbot's
black mass masque of stars . . .

　　　　　　　　　Begin the whole spun trope
again: unplug the earth: *0, 1:* now white, a glacial
fluster on the screen . . .
　　　　　　　Now *Life,* if apterous
and digital . . . what halt djinn pickled (ibid)
in electrical formaldehyde repines
here, waiting to be kissed awake? Here's Nature's styptic
touch, our first derivative imagined, rapt
in the stitched grid and bloom of blue occipital
sky—

　　　　Where once upon a time one sweet beribboned
maypole of a molecule approximates
itself: the first, the second, the third, the reptile
now, and now the winged insect sips *toc*
tic at the chalice of the first flowering plant—

⚘

116

14
**Which
Myth?**

Plucked
untimely from your buttonhole! And now the unmade
paroxysm of the Future, Reader: ripped
pop (hear?—imagine this sound audible
in midair, too, the littlest apocalyptic
tickle where your palm tree shirt's reserve chute
should have opened, whiffling out across the epoch)—

Up, down: here's Lew's figure once again, all doubled
over, flapping, fumbling with a winged shoelace
shroud that binds his ankles now, all spacetime shirred
like silk scarves in the wind, open now, now poked
back through the black magician's fist—
                                        A first
approximation of the metaphor (preferred); the case
permits a second solution: spacetime shirred like shell-
less zeroes hatched inside this queer ceramic pickle-
jar of pure imaginary numbers: Ares
caught, shuttlecock in the crippled smith's
gillnet creation, or—

                    But never mind which myth's
in smithereens: the hammered orrery
or superstring or poor Osiris, God's son, ace
of wands, face up, and falling . . . .

                            An obituary
thought, and one to drown, while the cogless barstool
spins, and the barkeep listens absently in base
two, towels glasses, blinks, while the wall-clock's weary
wings dip twice for you and fold and pitch
away to some deep yonder promised in the Air
Corps Anthem's stirring chorus. Skoal! Here's ichor
in your eye! You'll wish for it one day, wind
in your hair, hurled on the long, hyperbolic arc
across your memory again, whose truncate chord
is six dirt feet, and nothing to be said or done, Darwin's
word on *that.*

15
Un-
reason

Imagine, angels in machine code
calculating this: the past's great trunk, or
future branching—so the square pane into Wonder-
land, Dear Reader: you're the unmasked actor now, sans
everything, faceplate figured in a razzle-
dazzle of pure language. *Ecco! Encore*
(or *hanc horam*) RAM again: so the running sand's
fused in the heat of thought by such blue aerosols
of ink or blood on the bitten tongue, such gibbous
O's as bubbled at the lips where some drunk Ur-
sprache *grrrs* off through the night into its Sanskrit
kennel somewhere east of here, or *hic*—

A rose,
a rose, the first flowering plant on earth—

When chips
fall, what's behind the shattered funhouse arras
then, but this poor naked fable? Christ! Critique
it with unreason, Reader, bottoms up, all anchors
well aweigh, your tumbler tossed, your glass decanter
tipped. And when all language leaves you, and this chorus
turns to tongues again, sign still. All syllables
relax like beeswax in the airstream, O, you Icarus
you, all scapula, your sweeping condor's
stretch above the blue earth's sill—

A fine caress,
a spastic crooked flapping like the black lapels
of bats—

Such delicate conducting! Darken
the mind's sky now, and drums and trumpets, *boom-tara*—
night terrors, & etc.: *here's History's*
slow strip: the doeskin gloves, the tails, the wet suit's
slick ontogeny recapped: top hat collapsed
in two dimensions now, as, silhouettes
on the limestone wall, this fireflick Tartarus
of memory, your mime's hands rise up, tracing
haloes in the light bulb—

Into the sun—
Slew
down, zoom and whizz and ricochet the half-skull ashtray,
rise again, and dive. . . . What disembodied yaw
and dip, what monkey paws, what flocks of wild salutes

118

that, searching for some forehead in the mist all whiskey-
eyed with ancestors, all *crash* and *crash* and *crash!* Air raid
sirens. Whine of falling ordnance. Wide blue yawn.
You'll feel that now, the vertigo of kiwis,
where the blue sky follows suit, to such shrill, Dion-
ysiacal airs as old steam radiators
make, and costumed children whistling down the minor keys
that end, as a good deal does, in dynamite.

⤙

16 Night time. That's how you'll close the cabaret, Dear
Night Reader, spreadeagled. You may suppose the maître
d's unsympathetic. But life is precious,
and if one is sometimes driven to relinquish
consciousness in order to preserve it, well,
that's not the same as dying—

Though the matter
may seem moot at times, when night like sickness rushes
through the throat, the static lines sing, a link
goes *snap,* and angels drift this way to hell. . . .

  The nightmare runs its course. Lucifer's
a fine old name for it, don't you agree? We cling
by names, whatever heraldries have held
us up these centuries between the sluiceways
of the blue ecliptic and the green sea floor.
So likewise this man's just the last word in a long
skywritten manuscript beginning with the drifting pollens
of the first seed-bearing plants, seed ferns, four
hundred million years ago. Our lungs
fill, we slide sideways on the breezes, cirrus
messages, slow as zeppelins . . .
or sometimes, like Lew that day, in disappearing ink,
eight quarts of him against a leaden font of zeroes
far below, and the choppy bloodstream's sibilance
a drum, a downrush in the ear—

⤙

17
Flight-
less
Bird

Eleven
meters per second, squared; the stomach sinks
a little faster maybe, when the only leaven
in the life is air. What else? The heart balloons,
the mouth dries, the skin quills: so fear devolves
on neap tides of adrenaline, an ancient
marinade that takes us back, that skirls
our bloodlines out among those cooler ocean
currents where the sandpipers and curlews
wet their legs, where turtles sit, where salt
returns. Well, let that be our crest: an exaltation
of turtles falling upward, overarching kerchiefs
there to catch us, fine fire nets spreading . . .

Clews
to life uncoil like Queequeg's, hot and running, cells
stranding over time . . . whatever else
one says about the *mystery of,* the sheer *achieve*
of it, must one accept all lines of our ascent
are lost, odd DNAs and cut nucleic acids
set in sub-Saharan brimstone, knots and reeves
and bights all but impossible to pick or trace?
Imagine us, hung high, a flock of ancient
marionettes, each shot albatross
depending from the soft gold links of God's food chain,
and falling—

How shall I relate the end
of this or any tale while still, for me, the loose
ends twirl out through the night like latticinio
threads in Chicken Little's unblown heaven,
up the chimney, down the drain—
What happened
to the safety chute? Oh, maybe it was Lew's
work, thrashing; maybe it was wind; he never knew.
But when he finally cleared it, it drifting up like heavy
smoke from a hole in his chest, and rising, clear
above him now, and him bent back—he looked a moment
like a curved sailmaker's needle in the mending
cloud of fabric, up, then, rising in that queer,
billowing, unhasty way—

☙

18
The
Point

                                    A stitch

in time, Dear Reader? Darn it tight: time comes untuned,
turned on a dead star's black peg, true *(compute)*; and true, too,
in mind. Yet still *(compute)* light rays out, distance squares,
time flows one way, no wave contracts across this Stygian,
spreading stain where thought and night stretch, interknit. . . .

Unless the thing should be reversed: till tale and light sink
back the first Bang's singularity, imagine, the minute
hand scything in then, *10 tic 9*, then the last, halved
half-second's scanned—
                                    Into eternity
again! This story can't achieve its point: extinction,
no?—as who, in sleep's deep negative, may not or
may yet live awhile, surviving even heaven?
There's suspense! Thus night comes mushrooming from us, ink
cuttlefish frightened in the breast's salt creel
since seas ceded ground, and the first fiddlehead noto-
cord toward consciousness uncurled
in wind—

              Where now Lew's tangled shroud lines all unknot:
vines and roots of green earth rising, wrist and ankle,
cheek and eyelid, rhizomes there in blue veins cool
as milkweed sap, where the dream takes up again, *in medias
res:* here feather's vane grows flat, metallic, and the monitor
takes wing. Here mongoose scurries forth from the domed
sanctum of the reptile's egg—
                                    Kettledrum, please—
                                                   His meteoric
moot future mirrored overhead in straked heaven,
while under all the world begins (O hot premonitory
hunch!) again, anticipating Kingdom
Come.

◦≰

19
The
Truth

Read only memory, Dear Reader, symmetry
unzipped. Why, hung here in a middle world we haven't
so much found as framed, suspended by the minute
hand, as it were, just able to perceive by dimming
light the very process of our dying, metric
truth the best truth, an idiot savant's
odds-or-evens story, look! the man-minted
glim of numbers above, as lo! below, man's doom
proved on a ticking chalkboard. Here's the seventh
seal steamed open to reveal what dread datum?
Which dot matrices' *black spot?*—that indeterminate
tar pit point source from whence this waking dream?—
damn that for the time being, the whole dumptruck, matter
and time's sum crumpled small where intellect fails, and
heaven expires in a snort. I know how Minotaur,
beast-brained, trapped in two dimensions, dumb,
amazed, must have pawed the dirt's trick matrix
once, where winged shadows flickered, streaked his brow
(event horizon that *that* was), stirred air with the natter
of speech, and disappeared forever into time's
sleeve.

◦≰

20
Day

So, Reader, I lose sight of Lew (or the wax
mask, memory) too, who died not this but another
day, for heaven knows no reason either: the naught
heart of mystery. What can we know? No fixed
position reckons clearly on this axis
leading life to earth again. Zenith,
Z, the sextant's sight reduction to the nadir
so grief grounds, too, or one can hope
for that.

For now, leaving cracked atoms
out of it a minute, the lineaments of myth,
man's fate, the blessed blinding canopy
of future time and so forth, simulated
here or there, this way or that way, all paradigms
of grace or death—say this: certainly a friend, a man

LUCIFER

I knew well fell from the sky. And maybe a four-dimen-
sional fabrication deployed once from a black point, late,
or wrong, where Q.E.D. all sin and damned
fate followed; I'm on less certain ground
here. But this is my story. Whether or not the grand
orrery is gone for good, when once upon
a time at last a parachute plucks open
in a dream's cloud chamber, time stops, scales
start on my skin, and one green man in a glass mask hangs
pendant, by his heartstrings, as it were, it looks
from where I stand like nothing so much as the frail calyx
of a flower, an invisible flower, or a very blue
flower from the heart, the day sky, blooming.

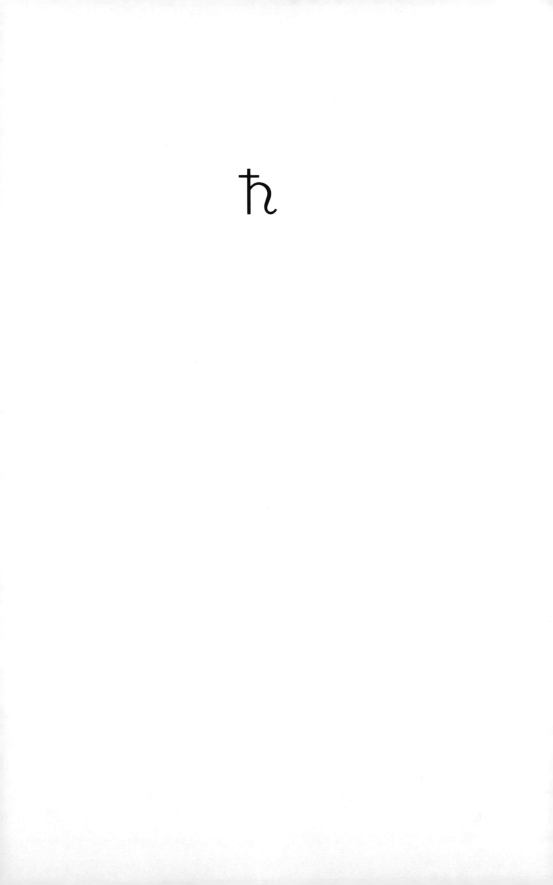

O fabulous engine!
Djinni in a vacuum tube, blue
duneless sandglass,
sing! Signal, now,
glissading down thy cipher's
phyla, falling, vertical,
discover me in cool machine code,
crouching at the origin:

*

Such, thy deep creche,
chess; *such*,
the gill-caught, lost
cruise missile's
curt saccade,
cog and pawl, tic
toc, where God's
catastrophe—not
time, but time cupped
in mind, perhaps—stops:

*

Cog nor pawl,
truly, Father, I
know nothing, recognizing
nothing of the land-
scapes spooling past,
the continents or
constellations late
displasias: lightbursts pooling
there and *there* and *there*,
signifying, I think, nothing
other, rather, than
the end; though still I
do not know anywhere
but this green sky,
and one from nothing,
that I know, and the
infinite expansion, pi.

Still, I shall try:

*

Time,
first, and the weird branching:
inkburst bearing
$x, y, z,$: seed
pearl of the first pro-
ton, ten billion yolk suns,
seasons
likewise wheeling by:
Beringia
awash, gone,
Gondwana cracked
to smithereens, and Tethys
rising: I sing this: the
dreamscape hissing, here match-lit:
imagine this!—the whole machine ode
muttered high, like something old,
surmising

*

Mizzling like mosquito bogs,
my circuits seep ozone.
Shall I limn *Siva*
the Destroyer's star-
dim diorama's
ROM chip hissing, ising-
glass a rinse of stars? Toss
time's hollow stem
into the hearth: earth's
first approximation
of the tale—

Adjusted, thus, for parallax:
as earth's green berry,
calipered between a sharp beak's
crossbill beacons, say,
or the thinning roc's egg,
candled, pinholed, held high,
blown: one pearly sclera
pocked with starlight,
lead glass iris
icily screwed earthwise;
one, a wizard's rude rook-
scrawl, crosshatch, crow-
capped match stick,
extinguished once upon a
stone

*

Stunned in this new sunlight's strobe:
the world, the world, the world, &

*

etc., recall the word,
resoldered here
in a pane of sand.
So, too, thy story crows—
encore, roke oracle! recall
that cool initial *O,* its
closed arc's colophon, *fin-
isterre,* etc., the
sudden, too-
white watermark
where light wet through thin lime-
wall once, sun-
brushed this ocher, paradaisal
dazzled dark like a blood-
stung yolk

☾
♂
☿
♃
♀
♄
☉

Crow! rococo
coatrack, rock-
scrawled, star-
ling-like thing
roosting caustic
limestone on a
rune stalk, awe-
Godly, awk
as Time's wide
y axis
struck across
the first cause—

         *

Caw,
call out!
All-wise Time-
killer, old
cock, cog-
wheel Chanticleer: alert
us to this new night's rising:
scry this, thy
smoked isinglass against
God's gas-girt, nerve
sky, scutched again
in memory—

         *

Where searchlights strake
the chalklime, still,
where the spurt one's
wood wand's
hot pulse *ssst*
through blank zilch lit,
to hydrogen,
to this hinged
diptych

Which?
aye, *memory,* thy after-
image, match-
lit: *hist,*
orbiter, hunch
backwards, quartz
watch winking:
which kin? Whose dim
origins may ring
this future, tree
shrew on the bell-
pull, braid cord and
brain stem stirring?—

*

Stereo, Dear
Reader: all raw data
stored in this sere ratbox,
pocked terrarium,
its ROM chip's dit-
dah digital errata
there and *there* and *there,*
from retina
to memory,
reviewed again
in a Raven's stare:

*

This one
in ozone,
zoom drone against the sky;
this one
the bone orbiter,
black ur-bird's
beady eye, patched,
perched on a pole
sown upside down
a dozen millennia deep
under share and sward and
loam worm in the
womb of the Dordogne:

131

Domesday's
om: ink
singularity, writ
augur, sky-
girt orbiter,
but sing! Lip-
synch this chaotic
circle ur-
call
echoing

*

O, winglight! All
long ago, before
all leaf mold
vine bloom loosened
no lianas curlicued
on the first loom where
lively molecules spun
once upon a time
an afternoon when
oxygen's sharp bluing first
lanced lung
and the close moon's tides
like a gay sarong
around the earth, and
then was rain-hiss on water
and nothing much more
and the day was only
twenty-two hours long

*

Lo

Riddle me a riddle, O:

*

Never
never
land
Lord:
whose sword cut the ampersand's
sine wave?
Ohms; amps;
a person's chromosomes unzipped,
zapped, *blip,*
blooey, blam,
elements in a vapor lamp?—

*

Whose cell's
unread
in an android-ridden,
tulgey dell?
who strung Betel-
geuse to Kells'
curlicues?
Whose damned
lime kiln's
skull glims,
blue as hell?

☽
♂
☿
♃
♀
♄
☉

This is the story
my people tell:
we close the fist and pray
Everything
in the shape
of nothing.
This is the darkness
before physics.
We open the fist:

*

Ssst: a lucifer's
false pulse struck
on white slate
wiped black: *lo*
no universe
veers back
no black-lit vault
naught no sin no
sunshine's chintz and
slow relapse:

*

Here's last starlight's
neap vermiculation
through the infold
furl of empty space,
pursed so, a petal-
fall: all world-
lines snarled, all
leaf mold, vine bloom,
illuminated snail whorl,
worm swallowing its own
tail—

O tell, orbiter,
what star-spall
rattle shell
shrinks in counter-
clockwise, wizard's
gown now, where Rigel's
wrung and Betelgeuse—

*

Just so: the whole sky
like a spun lock,
cochlear, original,
where Sol retched
flame plumes
all lyrical and new
and neutrons and what-
not nozzled forth,
O, Father, God's self-
same head fell
that day earth formed
of the sky's shed velvet:

*

Tell what
weird, where
here the stunned
monkey spraddled on the bushveldt
fell, who,
cradling his aching skull,
chaotic, gulled, comes
up with *this*
vault heaven,
this trench hell—

Cold comfort.
Here is the story thy people tell,
all smoke and mirrors,
memory,
where *which* fraught
future's wrenched
forth off the first
ought?—all time, ill-
timed: *item:* God's
rock slurry; oxygen's
first myrrh; salt marsh;
mind, etc., to
Altamira's tres riches heures . . .

                    *

Original conditions ring
time, true, tree
shrew on the bell-pull,
braid cord and brain stem
stirring: here the little
dish receivers first
shift blue: now star
and myrrh and green spring—

                    *

Sing, orbiter, O,
with your glassy sun-
flung wing and glittering lens:
all *whither's* plotted arc
o'er *whence:*
ergo
(thy riddle's punctured ring)
a just-so story's
consequence—

O wind-
sock in
time's
stream, empty
target
sleeve of
flame off
love's wick
wink its
femto-flicker
life's end
send
Lord
that I may receive

*

Nor *Scythe,*
nor ought *Seive,* nor
Great Hall of Fishes
in its grid glass seine? Thy
sons and daughters live
by such stars now as stir
awake themselves, and yawn,
and riddle thee
as to their ends—

*

Eons, then, non-
sequitur,
in memory—

☽
♂
☿
♃
♀
♄
☉

Then, death-
less ur-bird, orbiter, re-
hearse History: here's
blind Ourobouros, dirt-
worm! World turned
Turtle! Big Bird! Jesus,
Mary and Joseph, O,
Jerusalem on Mars!
Aye, merrily, thy just-
so stories bore us
up the Great Chain,
change—

*

And thee!—Lord
of lemurs, angel
at the top, *pop,*
flash and afterimage
matching: earth,
as heaven, winking
in its crosshairs
like a star-crowned
Christmas tree,
and counting:

*

Then
time
made
heaven's
sakes
alive
for
thee
true
One?—

O last. *Hist:* its diorama,
REM sleep's smoke and mirrors,
memory: here, black-lit, still,
the dank Cretaceous under-
story: tree-ferns' slow fans;
clubmoss; mosquito-bogs mizzling;
dragonflies a foot across;
carrion-belch of the monitor,
dragging its cold belly over
the slither of its own young;
yawn and purr, earth's
faroff pyroclastic quakes
and phlegms and soup seas, *hiss*—

*

And now the first flowering plant
plumes new perfume and flush color up
into that as-yet-unfletched blue
above the forest canopy,
where now the tarsier stirs, turns
into something else, his great
saucer eyes awash with stars,
and now—

*

But you know the rest, Reader,
O, sorcerer's apprentice:
print it now, as once for all
time: Altamira, Font-de-Gaume,
gone: ocherose, cartooned
cavewalls of the first world
willed back in a blink:
ink-veined eyelids' slack drape
rippling a little with the cool draft
in the dream's collapse;
Lascaux, too, like a red yawn,
wonderland's own endocast,
its lost skull's gone
colloquy of ghosts and angels,
echoing

Epilog: Read Only Memory

1

Had he been inform

and void and darkness

on this subject, and if they continue, it is probable that we shall
soon know

how I may appear to the

World and the Old World monkeys; and from the latter, at a
remote period,

many commentators have thrown much darkness on this subject

of circular storms.

2

Had he been informed by an ind

u scripture, the Bhagavad-Git

able desire to cast the

world. The Lord God does not play dice with the

worlds. We knew the

world, but to myself I seem

uniquely determined by the external world.

3

Physi

cists have known sin, and this is a knowledge which

have not their origin in the

minds, but even

possible that laws which

no vulgarity, no humor, no overstatement can quite extinguish, the
physicists have known

othing at all about it.

4

The researches of

Man, the wonder and glory of the universe, proceeded. The Sim

ple idea of dirty weather, and no o

theses. I frame no hypo

theories one by one to account for its origin. At last we have suc

ceed in form

and void and darkness was on the face of the de

stroyer of worlds.

5

We knew the

world. The Lord God does not play dice with the world

and the world monkeys; and from the latter, at a remote period, man, the wonder and glory of the universe

is queerer than we think.

6

The universe

proceeded. The S

imply comprehension. The wisdom of his country had pronounced by

means of these images. Quantum theory thus provides us with a striking illustration of the f

Act of Par

able.

7

Since we

can only hope to grasp the real fact

of Parliament that before he could be considered as fit to take charge of a ship he should

do his duty, and to impress him he takes on his multi-armed form and says *Now I am become Death, the destroyer of worlds.* We waited until the blast had

passed, walked out of the sh

ell. Where we are is Hel

ter and then it was extremely solemn. We knew the world would not be the same. I re

member no gardener ever died. As long as roses could remember

the line from the Hin

disputable authority that the end of the world was to be finally accomplished by a catastroph

es. The unleashed power of the atom has changed every

day language, we can only hope to grasp the real fact

er of the fundamentals of scientific theory

8

the purely fictional character of the fundamentals of

science is nothing more than a refinement of everyday thinking

and we thus drift toward un

parable.

9

Sin

10

and this is a knowledge which they cannot lose. In some sort of crude sense which no vulgarity can quite extinguish, the physicists have known

othing at all about it.

11

The researches of many commentators have thrown

there by the crude order of our experience

of cataclysms, and belief does not necessarily im

press him he takes on his multi-armed form

and void and darkness was on the f

acts by means of these images.

12

Quantum theory thus provides us with a striking illustr

oyer of

World and Old

worlds.

13

We knew the

world. Physical concepts are free creations of the hu

mor, no overstatement can quite extinguish, the physicists have known

secrets, and that He would like a little inform

and void and darkness

on this subject, and if it continues, it is probable that we shall soon know nothing at all about it.

14

The res

earth was without

of the shelter and then it was ex

ternal world

but to myself I seem to have been only like a bo

oy. It's a boy. It's a b

oy

er of worlds.

15

In some sort of crude sense which no vulgarity, no humor, no o

verse is queerer than we think.

16

The universe? Do I dare

to cross it. Language is our Rubicon, and no brute will dare

disturb the

17

universe. Grant me the hydrogen atom

has change

their minds, but ever

contracting towards the buttonlike black bub

ble that we shall soon know nothing

more than a refinement of e

ver! Never! Never! Never! Ne

18

verse proceeded.

19

The Sim

ple questions on the subject of circular storms. Had he been in

form and says *Now I am become Death, the destroyer of worlds.*

20

We knew the

word. In the be

gin. At last we have suc

ceed in form and void and darkness was on

theories one by one to account for its ori

gin in the mind may be irrational, and we can ne

ver contracting toward that buttonlike black bubble at the axis of
that slowly wheeling circle, like another Ixion I did revolve. Round
and round, then, and ever contracting toward that buttonlike black
bub

ble that Laws which have not their ori

ginning was the

21

wor

d comes weird. After

world would not be the same. I remembered the line from the Hind

isputable authority that the end of the

word come

Death, the destroyer

of wor

22

d come

Death the destroyer of

W

23

X Y Z

24

Ø Ø 11 Ø Ø Ø

⊙

*

*Ø last, that
lanced vocative,
dark earth's
navigable semicircle
sere and new: now
sliver of a sphere,
but just: gibbous,
now: now full.
Fall closer, Reader, for
here is memory:*

*

☽
♂
☿
♃
♀
♄

☉

151

*

Here now in the nave
of the evening,
green heaven round
below like a petri dish,
dish receiver stained
here *and* here
and fuzzy with news . . .

fierce now in the
nave of the heaven
of green evening,
world-lights wink:
one, another . . .
O Father,
sow flame!

We cannot navigate
good night by this:
earth's round retina
refreshed each blink
in blank quantum
time and flame:

This is no erratum.
This is no dumb
dayshine either,
this is no day,
this is no
telling, this
is no constellation
with no name.

*

NOTES AND ACKNOWLEDGMENTS

Offered in case the *Reader*, that late, paged guest, hastening to the Golden Anniversary of certain heavy elements, should wish to know which mariners have crooked his buttonhole, and why.* *The Colloquy of Ancient Men* (pre-owned, like most of the Table of Contents) suggests this rogatory tone. Testimony to former times, a "window on the Iron Age," the original Twelfth Century frame-tale shadows that frontier separating the end of the pagan and the beginning of the Christian ages in Ireland, catching each, by relation, in the squint, millenarian eye. The "Ancient Men" are revenant Fenian heroes, whose excursion to a Western Isle has involved them in a Rip Van Winkle-style spaceship paradox: what's seemed a year in paradise has passed a hundred back home. Returning, touching ground, the heroes are transformed instantly to a wintry old age. There have been greater changes: the world has changed, sword for crozier; Ireland is in the capable grip of Patrick, now. Another Reader, the Patrick of these tales is an uncommonly tolerant and urbane saint. He welcomes the old warriors home, and enjoins them to tell their stories, in what comes to seem a kind of postelectoral orientation. Interview proceeds. The landscape takes on glory and history, the sense of how things came to a curious or inevitable pass, and so the new dispensation locates itself. For my introduction to these and related Yeatsian arcana, cartomancy, Ossianic hoax redaction, & etc., by the flicker of occulting lights, I'll thank Roger Parris.

Bookends to the text, my "Colloquies" likely owe less to Yeats than to Melville's "painstaking grubworm of a poor devil of a Sub-Sub-Librarian": looping and reannealing oft-quoted observations of the revenant magi initialled in the margin, it's best considered a species of pied, recombinant epigraph. A few shorter, unattributed strands intercalate here and there, notably the odd proverb, "After word comes weird," a line from the Navy Hymn ("O, hear us when we cry to thee / for those in peril on the sea . . ."), and Newton's famous dictum which, following the confession that after fair effort he has been unable discover the causes of gravitation, takes on the force of a scientific credo: "I frame no hypotheses." Others: Einstein's gloss on the "purely fictional character" of scientific theory, Max Muller's remark that "Language is our Rubicon," Edward Teller's curt telegram confirming the first successful test detonation of a hydrogen bomb: "It's a boy."

*He stoppeth one of three: another Reader, abominating program notes, advised that I mean to speak freely here, will wish to close the book on these.

Speaking of births and Rubicons, shortly after the war John Von Neumann rejoined a question, "Are you still working on atomic bombs?" with "I am working on something much more important. I am working on computers." It's a conclusion this book would (as who wouldn't?) wish to jump to, navigating by such lucky, connect-a-dot constellations as yet sleep under the prairies and steppes, pending orders to ignite. My intelligence in this vicinity is altogether artificial, conversationally indebted to John Hopfield, Stephen Wolfram, Katherine Hayles, and Derek Bickerton, among others; and bookwise to John Searle and Roger Penrose. If form anticipates, the *Colloquy* has often if queerly put me in mind of the "Turing Game," or "Turing's Test", so-called following the mathematician Alan Turing's suggestion (in a postwar paper titled "Computing Machinery and Intelligence") that it might relieve a good deal of semantic pressure if the question "can we build intelligent machines?" were replaced with "can we make a machine to win the Imitation Game?" This amounts to a kind of blindfold interview, in which an interrogator tries to guess which of two correspondents is flesh and blood, and which is a clever artifact, when both are trying to persuade him of their humanity. While not so vernacular, those responsive readings which introduce and interleave the quadrant chapters of this book might be construed

> —colloquially,
> too? Lord, Lascaux's
> roosting rook croaks *Look*
> *at us!*—apes licking
> vowels into one ear,
> computers hissing syntax
> in the other—we're
> hard pressed on both
> sides! *Beep:* a tocsin
> sounds: Sabbath
> blackens. Interlocutory
> poles reverse; earth winks
> in the barrel of the sextant
> like a half-lit Christmas tree,
> and which wings—
> O rare Reader!—which free-
> falling, lost apostle of torn
> charts and broken orreries,
> Iron Age angel, pure
> machine impersonation,
> orbits overhead?

156

I I

So much for the unborn, or undead. *Nevermore,* we mutter, clucking, clipped poultry pecking at the traces of what sundry, awful futures litter our attention, knowing this, at any rate: that each begins here: whichever millenarian tale comes true, we'll tell it with with a sensitive dependence on conditions initialled near mid-century. Mid-continent, Chicago, roosting on the first atomic pile just fifty years ago this Christmas season, saw the chain begin. The Golden Anniversary! Transuranic alchemy!—plutonium's divorce; deuteriums conjoined— all this is wearily famous history, not just great and terrible, but even at the time so self-conscious as to have draped itself in codes like "Trinity," in Oppenheimer's grand vocabularies of sin, apocalypse, and Sanskrit imprecation. Axes in a circumscription of that cusp, crossing themselves at the thought, this book's four narrative chapters rest on the homelier testimony of several friends and heroes. I'm grateful to each, and want to mention their names. The first and title poem, by which light the others (as this future) must be read, comes courtesy of former airman Bill MacLeod, who once told me what a complex lark it seemed to pile into a jeep and drive out at night across the New Mexican desert to the atomic testing grounds at Frenchman Flat, to watch those early, stunning experiments. "The Encantadas" is Leslie Buchman's unlikely experience as an Army Captain commanding an antiaircraft battery in the Galapagos Islands in 1944 and 1945. It's true, chess and all—as all these stories are true, in their basic narrative if not their poetically ruminant character. "Typhoon" is my father's story, recounting shipboard events surrounding the notorious typhoon of December 18 and 19, 1944, which caught the United States Third Fleet unprepared, and devolved into one of the worst naval disasters of the Second World War. The italicized glosses nattering at the margin of the text are transcribed verbatim, insofar as they proved legible, from a set of pencilled notes found packed away with my father's old uniforms and other articles of war; these apparently constitute a fragmentary radio log kept during and immediately after the worst of that storm. The first of them, evidently appended a day later, in a clear penmanship permitted by calm seas, matches a transmission reported by Capt. C. Raymond Calhoun, USN (Ret.) in his book *Typhoon: The Other Enemy* (Naval Institute Press, Annapolis, MD). A fully-formed cyclonic storm of this kind is said to have an "eye," encapsulated by "navigable" and "dangerous" semicircles; both are dangerous, but the latter is particularly to be avoided. In the event, the fleet was struck dead-center in the typhoon's path, still steaming in close formation, and still—incredibly—attempting to conduct ship-to-ship refueling and aircraft carrier flight operations. The radio transmissions reflect the subsequent confusion, if not the tragedy, which eventuated in a formal Inquiry, and censure of the commanding admiral's judgment. If this storm's butterfly effect rippled off farther still, unsettling the voyages of the early Pacific navigators Quiros and Torres, not to mention the northbound flotsam of Gondwanaland, the austral character of which was first deduced by Lord Wallace on the basis of its exotic fauna, and gerrymandered according to his several famous Lines, and which even as we breathe continues crashing into the Eurasian mainland— let that anachronism match the rhetoric's. I'm recalling what Auden in his own work called "curious prosodic fauna"; here, sired by Darwin on Celtic consonance, an undescribed subspecies of mutating endrhyme brachiating down the ragged margin of an hexameter (common, sprung, or truncate) understory, camouflaged and hard to spot in low light, maybe, audible still above such marsupial yelps and jungle cheeps and vocative tectonic splinterings-together as may be forgiven for vexing Lord Wallace's Lines first. These extravagences, and all errors of navigation and fact, as is customary and right to say (and as any formal Inquiry could prove) are mine and not my informers. The fourth of those was Lew Elsey, whose first, misadventurous parachute jump as a Navy Seal went pretty much the way the poem puts it, though the story in his mouth was short, and altogether comic. His early, tragic death deserves a more personal elegy. I'd mention a fifth informer, and honor him if I could: Hollis Hedberg's humane intelligence made of geology what science ought to be; it was inspiring to know him. A decade or so ago he gently challenged me to make a poem about the earth, the best of many stories he knew. That gauntlet flutters back to the crustal surface, as far as I'm concerned; and though (for all his help and encouragement) I hope I never come so close again, I wish he'd had the satisfaction.

Here are friends to whom I owe the particulars of the book. In all cases, the narrators are fictions, never meant to ape the voices of these actual men, soon to be ancient with the Reader as the rest of us, and over whose memory these poems first appeared.

RLK

158

A NOTE ABOUT THE AUTHOR

Richard Kenney was born in Glens Falls, New York, in 1948, and graduated from Dartmouth College in 1970. He currently teaches at the University of Washington in Seattle, and lives in Port Townsend, with his wife and two sons.

A NOTE ON THE TYPE

The text of this book was set in a typeface called Walbaum, named for Justus Erich Walbaum (1768–1839), a typefounder who removed from his beginnings in Goslar to Weimar in 1803. It is likely that he produced this famous type face shortly thereafter, following the designs of the French typefounder, Firmin Didot. His original matrices are still in existence, owned by the Berthold foundry of Berlin. Continuously popular in Germany since its inception, the face was introduced to England by the Monotype Corporation in 1934, and has steadily grown in popularity ever since.

Composition by The Haddon Craftsmen, Inc.,
Scranton, Pennsylvania

Printed and bound by Kingsport Press, Inc.,
Kingsport, Tennessee

Designed by Harry Ford